The Flame

of

Beauty

Culture

Love

Joy

by

Torkom Saraydarian

THE AQUARIAN EDUCATIONAL GROUP

Post Office Box 267 • Sedona, AZ 86339

ISBN No. 0-911794-02-6

© 1980 by Torkom Saraydarian
All Rights Reserved
Library of Congress Catalog Card No. 80-67681
Printed in the United States of America

Typography by Modern Linotyping, Los Angeles
Printing by Bradshaw Bros., Los Angeles

Dedicated to
my beloved teacher
Hovhanes Chelebian
(Bola)

CONTENTS

ABOUT THE AUTHOR

Torkom Saraydarian has made a life-long search for unlocking the mysteries of man. His efforts have taken him to monasteries, ancient temples and mystery schools, to the churches and priesthood, to esoteric schools and organizations in different lands.

With candor and clear observations, the essential lessons available in all manner of teachings are evident in his writings along with inspiring and practical hints for manifesting the deepest truths concerning man's reality.

OTHER WORKS BY TORKOM SARAYDARIAN:

The Science of Becoming Oneself
The Science of Meditation
Cosmos In Man
Christ, The Avatar of Sacrificial Love
The Bhagavad Gita
    translated from the original Sanskrit
The Fiery Carriage and Drugs
Love, Freedom, Beauty, Joy
The Hidden Glory of the Inner Man
The Legend of Shamballa
Triangles of Fire
Five Great Mantrams of the New Age
The Hierarchy and the Plan
The Unusual Court
Symphony of the Zodiac

i

PREFACE

One day I was playing tag with three of my friends in the woods when a stranger approached. He was about 35-40 years of age, tall and handsome with very loving eyes. He sat down 15-20 yards away from us and we continued playing.

After watching us for awhile, he called my name and asked me to come closer to him. I went without hesitation and stood in front of him.

"What if I show you a game we can all play together?" he asked.

"How is it done?" I replied.

"I will show you." And we walked toward my friends.

Then he said to all of us, "We will play a good game, which none of you will forget." And he drew a large triangle in the soft earth with a dry branch. He then told each of us to stand on a corner. Then turning to one of my friends he said, "You are Joy." Then he turned to my other friend and said, "You are Love." And pointing his hand to me he said, "You will be Beauty. I will be Flame, and I will stand at the center of the triangle. Now see how we will dance. First we will be in total silence. Watch what I will do, then I will tell each of you what you are to do."

We kept total silence and he began to sing UR UR UR (which means fire) and with an exciting rhythm, he danced turning 360 degrees and then reversing it. The movements of his hands symbolizing a flame raising up from the earth to Space.

Then he turned to Joy and said, "When I say 'UR,' you will open your arms and say 'Joy,' feeling that my fire is inspiring joy within all your being. Let us do it . . ."

After a few minutes, he turned to Love and said, "You will do a similar thing. When I say 'UR,' and he says 'Joy,' you will add 'Love,' opening your arms horizontally and bringing your palms upon your heart, and turning around once as you say 'Love.' "

iii

And after a few minutes of doing this with him, he turned to me and said, "You are Beauty, and after I say 'UR' and after he says 'Joy' and after he says 'Love,' you will say 'Beauty' and your movement will be as follows . . ."

He closed his eyes, grasped his hands over his head and like a pendulum went right to left, left to right, while circling from left to right 360 degrees.

After showing this to us he said, "Now every movement will be rhythmic and synchronized. When I turn 90 degrees, you, Joy, will do one whole movement. When I do one round, you will have completed four movements."

And turning to Love, he said, "You, Love, will do four movements as you turn exactly with the speed I turn."

Then he turned to me saying, "You, Beauty, every time I turn 180 degrees, you will do one whole movement and you will turn exactly as I do."

After explaining all this to us, he gave us the note on which we had to sound our words, or our names. When all of us sounded them, it was a chord that touched our hearts. Then he added, "You feel that joy is transforming you. You feel that all creation is love. You visualize that all nature is singing beauty with the stars, and I will increase your fire with the Divine flame."

We started . . . with pauses and explanations and corrections. When we learned how to do it, we performed it seven times, then we sat in our corners, totally uplifted and energized. He got up and said, "Peace be with you," and walked away . . . we were motionless for a long time.

I wrote this book in gratitude to him. May peace be with him.

T.S.

Chapter 1

BEAUTY

I

*"With beauty we conquer.
Through beauty we pray
In beauty we are united."*[1]

NE OF OUR RECENT philosophers said that the purpose of life is survival. It seems to me that survival sub-stands all phenomena and that life does not pursue survival, because no matter what form life is in, *It ever is.* It is the form-side of life which tries to keep itself as it is, and which struggles to survive. This approach to survival is a hindrance on the path of life, in the long run. The form tries to prevent the free flow of life and its progressive unfoldment which is accomplished through the process of building and destroying the form.

It seems to me that the purpose of life, on any level, is the expression of Beauty, and this is especially true of the human kingdom. Man is created to manifest beauty. Man is created to enjoy the beauty of lower kingdoms, to be inspired by the beauty of higher kingdoms, and to synthesize these two beauties. In so doing he becomes a path between these two worlds of beauty.

1

When survival is emphasized people will do almost anything to "achieve" it. And when they achieve it they will see that they have always had it.

In the name of survival many crimes are committed: fear, greed, hatred, war. These are the foundations upon which modern man's psychology is based.

In the name of culture, creativity, and beauty, no crime can be committed. These are the fruits of the Spark in man who survives all decay, all change, and reveals to man through the expression of beauty THAT HE IS.

Beauty is the expression of that which survives through all levels of Divine manifestation.

Awareness of immortality, awareness of existence as a spiritual being, as a spiritual individuality, is achieved through creativity. Creativity is the labor to manifest the Inner Beauty—to manifest the Self—in outer expression.

As you manifest your true Self you manifest beauty because the Self is a wave in the ocean of the Cosmic Self, which is the Artist responsible for all manifestation. You, as a wave, carry on the creativity of the Cosmic Self to the shores of expression.

The urge to manifest beauty is not only human. It is the urge of all kingdoms and of all living forms: the atom, the cell, the crystal, the seeds of all kinds of flowers, trees and vegetables, the animals, birds, and superhuman entities such as our Planetary Life, Solar Life, and life beyond that. Through all these lives runs the spirit of the creative urge to manifest beauty. Each kingdom on each level, progressively aspires towards beauty and towards the manifestation of greater beauty.

Each life is supposed to radiate itself. Radiation is the expression of the beauty within each life. Flowers, birds, trees, animals, and even tiny insects have a tremendous drive toward beauty. Actually they are attracted to each other through expressed beauty.

You feel that a lily or a rose is proud of its color and form; you feel that the pine tree is proud of the beauty of its branches, its fragrance, its color, its psychic radiation.

A bird with its colorful feathers, pouring forth its own melody . . . a tree blossoming in the springtime and laden with fruit in the fall . . . a girl with her crystal purity and striving . . . a mother with her child . . . a man with his drive to serve and sacrifice—all are expressing beauty, radiation—but beyond these, I feel that the Great Lives of the stars and galaxies are laboring to produce Symphonic Beauty in Space.

Inspired men tell us that God sings, and all comes into existence as manifestations of His Song. What a magnificent way to say that beauty is the act of the manifestation of God's Purpose! Beauty is the result of the progressive adaptation of the form to the *Divine Intent*. All flowers, birds, trees, men, solar systems, galaxies are the result of the manifestation process of His Song.

It is only man who can be a conscious expression of beauty, or a distorter of beauty. As he harmonizes all his life to the Divine Intent, to the law of evolution and to the achievement of perfection; as he passes from glory to glory, from partial beauty toward total beauty, he becomes a conscious expression of beauty. This can be accomplished by first establishing communication, and then fusing with the Source of Beauty within himself.

In our physical, emotional, and mental consciousness we distort the beauty in nature with which we come in contact. We distort it because of our glamors, our illusions, and our selfishness.

Beauty evokes a synthetic response from all parts of our nature. This response may be joy, an expansion of awareness, a feeling of freedom, or a sense of synthesis and unity. It may surge through us as a feeling of deep gratitude, admiration, and a fiery aspiration toward purity.

Beauty works and stands only for unfoldment, release, evolution, and spiritualization. It expands our consciousness, enabling us to contact the transpersonal Self within us. The transpersonal Self is the embodiment of beauty, it is the Soul. Its nature is Love-wisdom, and beauty can be totally enjoyed only through the sense of Love-wisdom. Just as our body needs food, water, air and light, so our Soul needs beauty to unfold and to radiate. *Beauty is the path to Cosmos.*

Once we enter into the Soul consciousness, we will begin to see things as they really are. This means that we will see the archetypal blueprints of the existing crystallized forms. Beauty is the archetype, the Divine blueprint, the idea conceived in the Mind of God.

The transpersonal Self tries to bring into our consciousness the sense of beauty, and to establish the rhythm of beauty within us.

To manifest beauty we must expand our consciousness into the Soul consciousness, and contact the beauty in the Soul, through the soul. As we grow toward Soul consciousness we manifest more beauty because we harmonize our life-expression with the existing archetypal beauties. Each time a man contacts his Soul, he is charged with a stream of beauty which bestows upon him joy, upliftment, peace, and serenity.

The Soul is only a path leading us to deeper beauty, which exists in the sphere of the Spiritual Triad and beyond. There, we are closer to the Divine Melody and to Divine Energy.

True beauty inspires in us the qualities and activities which lead us into striving, expansion, self-observation, harmony, gratitude, and sacrificial service. All these are flowers on the tree of beauty, or notes in the symphony of beauty.

Beauty is materialized love. Love is the Essence of life. Any time, anywhere, when true love expresses itself, you have beauty. Love becomes beauty through manifestation of the archetypes, and the expression of love is the process of the adaptation of matter to Spirit, the expanding love.

The transpersonal Self which sometimes is called the Solar Angel, is the tuning fork (the keynote) of beauty. A life lived in harmony with that keynote is a life of beauty. A life lived out of tune with that keynote is an ugly life in which life-energy has difficulty in forming better ways of expression. This is the cause of all suffering. Whenever we suffer, we must strive toward more beauty. This will create a healing process within our bodies. Health is the externalization of Inner Harmony, which is achieved when a man steps into the fifth Initiation, the door to the world of endless beauty.

Each time a man strives and records an achievement, he manifests more beauty. Beauty is the manifestation of our ever-widening field of achievement or unfoldment.

When I was a boy my mother read a story which I have never forgotten. It tells of a great artist who wanted to paint The Last Supper. He was seeking a man who could be used as the model for Jesus. At last he found such a man, a man of radiant beauty, and asked him to be his model. The man agreed and the painting was begun. Years passed and the same artist wishing to finish his painting, sought this time, a man to pose for Judas, the betrayer.

He searched for many days without success, until one evening he entered a place of revelry. There he discovered a man who reflected the psychology of a betrayer, and asked him to be a model for the painting of Judas. The man agreed to go with the artist to his studio. As they entered, he began to cry bitterly. The painter asked,

"Why do you cry?"

Pointing to Jesus in the unfinished picture, he said,

"A few years ago, I was Jesus, and now I am Judas! I betrayed the beauty that was mine . . ."

Living according to the inner standards of simplicity, truth, and beauty makes a man the model for a great image. Living with an opposite attitude toward beauty, simplicity, and truth makes a man the model for a traitor.

Beauty is touched on a gradient scale. We may say that on the first level, the expression of beauty is a melody; on the second level it is a duet; on the third level it is a chorus; on the fourth level it is a Symphony. On the fifth, sixth, and seventh levels beauty enters into the domain of Eternity. It is about such beauties that mystics speak, describing them as ". . . beauties which cannot be expressed by words, but can be known only through direct experience." On all levels we have beauty, but the beauties found on the lower levels are constituent parts of greater beauties on higher levels. The search for beauty leads us to our Inner Self. The steps of the path leading to the Inner Sanctuary are built of living beauties. The Real Man is the beauty, and eventually it is this real beauty that will absorb the outer, suffering, faltering man into Itself. Then will the age-long labor to create beauty reach a new height, leading to greater beauty.

Each beauty is a center of energy. Every time we create, unveil, or identify with beauty, we build a radioactive source of healing, uplifting, unfolding, and purifying energy. We experience an amazing realization once we know that beauty is a charge of tremendous energy. It is as lightning, charged with the energy of the sun. Because of this, all creative people are filled with energy and radiation. This energy and radiation reach optimum expression when the Inner Sleeping Beauty, the Real Self of man, starts to awaken and shed Its light upon the surrounding world.

It is this awakening beauty which eventually forms the bridge leading to Eternity. After a man becomes a beauty unveiled, he has overcome death, and the matter side of life no longer has control over him. He passes from the inside to the outside to shed his rays of beauty, and to be a path which will lead men toward achievement. On this path he keeps his continuity of consciousness, and whether in the form or in the formless world, he stands as an ocean of beauty.

Striving toward beauty leads us to the future. Let us converse with our Solar Guide through words of beauty, and transform ourselves to a Chalice of beauty.

BEAUTY

II

Once i met an old man who was sitting on a river bank in a contemplative mood . He had a rosary in his hand and was rolling the beads between his fingers, saying for each bead in a very low voice, "Ya latif, ya latif."

After he was finished I respectfully approached him and asked "What does 'Ya latif' mean?"

With dreaming eyes he answered, "It is the name of Him Who is the end and the beginning."

"What does it mean?"

"The beauty . . . all beauty. Beauty in everything is Him." After saying this he entered again into contemplation. I sat there for a while. He was peaceful and in harmony with the river, with the trees, birds, and flowers. From that day on I felt a new sunrise of beauty within my heart.

Each man is a Spark or a Ray from that Fiery Source of all beauty. From that Source millions of years ago, each person was projected out into space as a Spark, and now is trying to go back Home to his Source through the path of beauty.

"O Thou who givest sustenance to the universe,
from Whom all things proceed,
To Whom all things return,
Unveil to us the face of the true spiritual sun
hidden in a disk of golden light,
That we may know the truth and do our whole duty
As we journey to Thy sacred Feet."

Beauty for human beings has these gifts:
1. Happiness
2. Joy
3. Bliss.

When the physical, emotional, and mental mechanisms are harmonized with the spirit, man feels happy.

7

When beauty touches the Soul and tunes it in with the Plan of the Hierarchy, all is in joy.

The Plan of the Hierarchy is the scale on which Purpose plays its music of beauty.

When beauty touches the *Essence*, the Self, man is flooded by ecstasy or bliss. Ecstasy is the moment when man and beauty become one, and it is that moment when the Purpose of life is unveiled.

When we see and witness any beauty we feel ecstasy, upliftment, great joy, and expansion. The reason is that through each beauty we touch Him. Through beauty we touch our own Essence, our Self. Through beauty the separate parts become One.

Ecstasy is a moment of unification with beauty. In ecstasy you transcend your personality level and change into a spiritual being, a being who is aware of the Source of all beauty. Thus through beauty you bridge the gap between you and Infinity.

Beauty is the expression in form of *intelligence, love, will*—in right proportion, and in harmony with the unfolding spirit.

All cultures of humanity are a progressive manifestation of beauty, a manifestation of the Essence.

There is no beauty without intelligence, love, and will. A real beauty manifests such powers and charges us with intelligence, love, and willpower.

Initiation is the gradual manifestation of Inner Divinity through beauty.

Creativity or expression of beauty is on seven levels:

1. Physical
2. Emotional
3. Mental
4. Intuitional
5. Atmic
6. Monadic
7. Divine.

Physical beauty is that which pertains to the body. The theory of evolution shows how our body became more and more refined and beautiful. In comparison to the cave man, half-animal and half-man, our modern humanity is exceptionally beautiful.

Beautification of our body is a continuing manifestation of our Essence until it becomes the expression of the living fire of

—Transformation
—Transmutation
—Transfiguration
—Sacrifice
—Resurrection.

Beautification is one of the phases of the physical body in the process of adaptation to the Divine Essence.

Emotional beauty expresses itself as right human relations, positivity, love, and magnetism.

Mental beauty expresses itself in creativity, the arts, and sciences.

Intuitional beauty expresses itself through divine faculties, higher psychism, purity, unity, striving, contact with the Plan and the Purpose of life.

Atmic beauty expresses Itself through power over the elements.

Monadic beauty expresses Itself as conscious immortality or continuity of consciousness.

Divine beauty expresses Itself as the ability to fuse oneself with all life, the whole life.

Our arts are accumulations of energy from these seven planes of fire. They evoke the corresponding fires and make them flow into our vehicles; causing purification, harmony, and transmutation.

Beauty evokes beauty, and the birth of beauty is the birth of Self, the manifestation of Self.

Beauty manifests in seven phases as the following:

1. In the form of architecture or sculpture
2. In sound and music
3. In color and painting
4. In movements and dance
5. In ceremonies
6. In speech or thought
7. In life or living.

On whatever level beauty is presented, on that same level does it create a point of awareness in those who appreciate it and enjoy it with all their hearts.

Beauty creates coordination in higher centers and uplifts the anchorage of consciousness from lower centers to their higher correspondences.

The purpose of beauty is to make the Essence of man come into manifestation, into birth. This is what true self-realization, or self-actualization is.

Self-realization can be achieved only when the Self becomes aware of himself through the mirror of his manifested beauty.

Creativity is a process of touching one's own Self; it is a moment of contact with one's own Self. The Self cannot be known unless it is manifested in creative action.

True art is the language of Self. Only art can create a contact between a Self and another Self. Art abstracts the consciousness from personality interferences and puts the individual Self in contact with another Self, or with the SELF. Only a true artist can reach the true Self of another person.

The greatest joy a person can experience is to contact the Self of another person through his own Self. Only true contact with the Self causes sublimation and harmonization within our vehicles. Any true contact with the Self releases a beam of light from the Self, and because of this ray, man becomes a guiding life, a source of strength for himself and others. This beam eventually turns into a path for others to travel toward their true Selves.

A rare beauty is mathematical. It is the synthesis of all equations which makes it irresistible. It can produce those balancing effects on the personality and the life for which the equation was designed.

To spread beauty is a heroic task. The army of ugliness is powerful. This army is composed of those who are in the trap of their maya, glamors, and illusions and are heavily loaded with karma. It is composed of those also who are consciously and unconsciously serving the involutionary forces, the dark brotherhood, whose intention is to retard the evolution of humanity. This army is well organized and has a powerful influence on money, politics, justice, and commerce. They use all possible means to fight against any organized beauty that is intended to lift up humanity as one race.

Their ugliness is expressed through literature, movies, nightclubs, houses of prostitution, gambling, drugs, acid and rock music, through many paintings, drawings, and illustrations.

Beauty opposes all these and indirectly hurts the business of the army of ugliness.

Ugliness fights:

—against purity
—against law and order
—against human rights
—against unity
—against culture and true education.

Whenever you see the distortion of beauty—stay away—because ugliness is malignant and it degenerates your system, your symphony.

Once a great Sage said, ". . . guard the heart." The heart is the temple of beauty.

Things that we do against our conscience create an irregularity of heartbeat and produce poison in our glandular system. Beauty is the best remedy to heal ourselves from irregularity of heartbeat and to purify our blood from the poison produced by our glands.

Through beauty we are polarized towards our higher Self, where we breathe the fragrances of goodness and truth. Those who are polarized towards beauty live a life of goodness, harmlessness, and truth because they are closer to their own Essence, to their own Divine nature. Such people are not affected by the urges and drives of the lower self, and that is the reason why they can live in goodness, truth, and beauty.

Identification with the lower self is the root of all evil because the lower self is not yet evolutionary; it is involutionary. The arc of involution is separativeness, materialism, selfishness, and totalitarianism.

Identification with the higher Self is the source of unification, spiritualization, selflessness, and creativity.

It is beauty that pulls you out of the lower self and fuses you with your true Self.

Beauty creates striving within you. No one can advance on the path of evolution, or on the path of perfection except through striving.

Striving begins the moment you contact a beauty and at the same time realize that your manifested life is far from being equal to that beauty. This challenges your spirit to gradually master your life and express beauty. Beauty sometimes reveals the imperfection of your nature, and you decide to change your nature through the inspiration of beauty. As one senses more beauty, his striving increases and his life changes into a life of discipline, into a process of harmonization with the inner vision of beauty.

Beauty releases joy. Joy is one of the best tonics to the nerves. Anytime you feel weak—create joy, increase joy. You will feel the increase of your vitality and this is the joy that manifests from beauty.

It is possible to cure many diseases with beauty. Even our eyesight improves by looking at and observing beauty. Our hearing improves when we listen to beautiful music. This is true of the other senses also.

Weakness of the senses is the result of partial withdrawal of the Inner Essence. Beauty attracts the Essence into the mechanism of the senses, and they improve immensely.

Even your mental activities increase in contacting beauty. Before taking examinations enjoy beauty, deeply feel the joy of beauty and you will see how much your intellect has cleared itself.

The weakness of mental powers is due to all those experiences which did not have joy in them. Such experiences hang on in your mental sphere and drain the vitality of your mental body. Joy disperses them and vitalizes the currents of electricity within your mind and brain. Open yourself to the joy of beauty.

Gratitude is the ability to see beauty in others. Every time you are grateful to someone you see beauty in him. And if you always live in beauty, you are always in gratitude. Gratitude is a great purifying energy which enables you to receive the impressions of great ideas and visions, without distortion, and allows you to be charged by those energies which can only contact pure vehicles. Gratitude is a unifying energy and through gratitude many gaps are bridged in man, in the family, and in society.

A young couple was seeking marital counseling. They said there was some coldness between them. After talking awhile I said, "Go and buy Walt Whitman's poetry, and every evening read it for one hour." They were wondering what poetry would do for them.

After one week the lady called me and said, "We are doing well. We are falling in love again."

Beauty awakens and strengthens the spirit of gratitude, and gratitude bridges the gaps. Gratitude is an appreciation of beauty.

Each beauty causes an expansion of consciousness—in those who attune themselves to that beauty.

Each beauty reveals new goals and visions towards which man strives.

Each beauty harmonizes the vehicles of the personality and lets the life flow and brings in greater health.

Beauty releases joy, love, gratitude.

Beauty makes a man generous and tolerant.

Beauty regenerates the secretion of glands.

Beauty creates right human relations, goodwill, understanding, universal harmony. It is so true that "through beauty man conquers."

Beauty creates *unity* because the Essence is magnetic. As you go toward your own Essence, you go toward the Essence of others. On the Essence level there is no separation, only unity.

How to approach beauty?

Beauty is everywhere. To enjoy beauty and use it as an agent of healing, self-transformation, and self-actualization, one must be aware of it and fuse with it.

Beauty always has an effect upon a human being whether he is aware of it or not, but conscious contact with beauty is a direct method to receive the full benefit of the charge. To have a conscious contact with beauty, people must be trained in the following points:

1. The object of beauty, in whatever form it is presented, must be observed very carefully. If you can touch it, you must touch it with your fingers, palms, face, even with your lips. You must come in physical contact with it, observing every sensation you are receiving from it.

2. If it is visual or auditory, concentrate your eyes or ears on the object in a deeply relaxed manner. See the shades of sound and color; the relations of notes or colors; the symbolic language they speak. Notice all your physical, emotional, and mental responses.

3. Then absorb the beauty into your being. Focus yourself and see the beauty in an inner sense. Hear the music as if it were play-

ing within you until the moment when you and the object of beauty fuse into each other.

4. The next step is to find the level on which the beauty originated. Uplift your consciousness to that level and try to find the real task of the beauty, the purpose for which it was created.

There were three boys passing through a gorge and they saw a beautiful waterfall—with pine trees at the top, many colors of the rainbow, little waterpools, eagles flying. They sensed the power of the falls, the serenity. Immediately when they saw it, they sat crosslegged on the grass in silence and watched the unique beauty of nature. None of them spoke. None of them moved until sunset, when with tears in their eyes they departed from the falls. That night none of them spoke. This beauty had such an impact on them that eventually it turned into a psychological experience.

The three boys became living fountains of creativity. One became a painter who thrilled people with his colors. Another one became a great singer and musician. The third one wrote books out of love for humanity.

Years later whenever they met one another, they hugged each other and remembered the waterfall experience. Then they departed in silence with a great creative tension. The experience turned into a living waterfall within these three creative boys who dedicated their lives to distributing beauty to all humanity.

Those who are sensitive to beauty know that any expression of beauty is part of the manifestation of the Cosmic Self, and is a creative process which is going on within the observer himself.

The waterfall was the action of nature, but it was also a key to unlock the Divine potentials within man and to release them in creative expression.

Beauty talks, if you learn its language. Behind the form, the eyes of the artist watch you. He imparts his concealed message to you, and if you surrender yourself to beauty, the artist turns on the living waters within your being.

Inspiration is the moment of contact with the Spirit of the artists. It is when the electric current of Purpose, of Plan, and ideation pours into your level of creativity.

The word "artist" is not usually defined in a proper way. An artist is a person who brings the Plan or Purpose of the Great Life into objectivity, thus building a bridge between humanity and its Source.

In this sense a politician can be a great artist when he tries to rule and to lead humanity to its highest good.

An educator can be a great artist when he tries to bring to birth the divine potentials of his students.

A philosopher can be a great artist when he tries to bring into our life the meaning and the purpose of existence.

An artist can synthesize all the efforts of the politician, educator, and philosopher in such a way that he inspires them with greater vision.

A scientist can be a great artist in the sense that all his discoveries are the laws and principles by which the Great Artist of the universe works. Science reveals the architecture within the beauty.

A religious man can be a great artist by trying to reveal the love and virtues of the Soul, and by building a ladder of ascent towards the ideal.

An economist can be a great artist in creating those ways and means by which the wealth of the planet can be enjoyed by all, and the standard of living can be raised to a new dimension for all.

5. The fifth step is to try to manifest the experienced beauty through your life expressions.

The music you heard, the poem you read, the painting you saw, the ballet, the opera you enjoyed must create a point of tension within you and eventually find an outlet in creative living. This can be done consciously by comparing your daily life with the point of tension you reached at the time of creative enjoyment.

The point of tension is on that level of consciousness or awareness where you were able to build an image of yourself in the fire of the creative enthusiasm, where you had a contact with your higher Self, and a glimpse of your future possible transfiguration while enjoying the beauty in ecstasy. In the light of this point of tension, you may transform your actions, your emotional expressions, your mental operations, your plans, your goals, and make them fit the frequency of your inner tension. Men of great honor, dignity, solemnity, and beauty are created when such points of tensions are sustained by them long enough to transform their lives.

6. The next step is to use your creative and inspirational moment as a means of service for humanity—radiating out the love, the beauty, the ecstasy, the light to all humanity—with the intention of healing the wounds of people; dispersing the clouds of hatred and separation and creating right human relations, goodwill, understanding; and a transformation of our social life. This step can be called the projection of beauty to the world.

Listening to uplifting music and at the same time visualize it as if it were sounding all over the world, inducing great harmony and rhythm in human life. See great colors and inspiring forms and project the beauty to all places where disharmony and hatred exist. Visualize the exciting changes occurring in those fields.

The art of the new age will have only one goal—to release the beauty, the Divinity in humanity, to heal the wounds of humanity, to create love, understanding, and harmony between all people in spite of all their differences.

It is true that with such a purification man will be able to tap the sources of greatest joy and bliss within himself.

You can share the moment of your ecstasy with those who are passing through critical moments of their lives. You can even bring "music" and "color" and "motion" into the minds of those who are caught in the hands of darkness, crime, and greed.

You can visualize such a person or such a group and see them enjoying the moment of ecstasy with you. As you go deeper into your creative and fiery enjoyment, visualize the change they are going through.

The great creative artists are the source of sanity, understanding, and health of nations. It is possible to use their creative expressions to transform our schools, our prisons, our offices, and our homes.

It is even possible to heal yourself through the forms of art. Beauty can be technically used in hospitals and in prisons to heal and change lives through scientific procedures. Remember that beauty is health. Beauty is power. Beauty is the greatest disinfectant and harmonizer.

In beauty you have the Presence of all that exists. To contact that Presence means to be a beauty. Beauty is a fountain of psychic energy.

Our children not only must be put in touch with beauty in their art classes, but they also must be taught how to see beauty, how to enjoy beauty, how to be beautiful. They must learn to see the beauty in flowers, in great rivers and waterfalls, in all forms of life, and to come in contact with the creative beauty of great artists.

7. The next step is an endeavor to find a balance in color, sound, form, and movement in whatever field we live or work.

A certain color enjoys certain music. Certain music enjoys certain movements of forms. How should a person arrange them, and in what number so that one is able to see his beauty in his field?

I was once sitting in a very simply decorated room. A beautiful girl in a long white dress played the piano for me. As she was playing I saw in one of the corners a wood carving of Krishna playing his flute. I noticed the drapes were violet, the carpet golden. All these fit each other and the music in such a way that I felt an extreme joy and an uplifting energy. I almost heard Krishna's flute with her music.

When she finished I said, "Your symphony was beautiful."

"Symphony?"

"Yes."

"Hmm."

Then suddenly she jumped up and hugged me and said, "Yes, I understand. You are referring to Krishna, to the curtains, to the carpet, to the piano, to the music, to me . . . all one symphony."

8. The next step will be to go deeper into your creative experience. Ask yourself if your creative work is a personal satisfaction or psychological release, or a forced labor for material needs. Or is it a planned creative action, through which you are trying to cooperate with the Great Nature to achieve its continuous birth, the continuous manifestation of its true Self. Through your creative work are you trying to release the imprisoned seeds caught in glamors, illusions, and maya, to free the hidden beauty in each living form?

Is your creative work bringing more sanity, causing greater healing and cooperation among people and nations? Is it enlightening the minds of the human race?

Is it helping to improve our political, economic, and social conditions; or is your "creative work" an expression of your inner wounds, depressions, obsessions, and a means of satisfying your greed, hatred, fear, and pride?

A creative artist has a compassionate heart—full of wisdom and the spirit of sacrifice. The heart of a true artist is in tune with the hearts of all manifested lives.

Once a great Sage said, "Repeat Beauty again and again, even with tears, until you reach your destiny."[2]

BEAUTY

III

In each human being exists a Spark of that Wholeness, of that Creative Center and harmony, "from Whom all things proceed, to Whom all things return." This is the Central Fire discussed in many cultures. Each human is a Spark of this Ocean of Fire in whom the All is found as a microfilm. This "microfilm" is a creative spark, as its Source is, but is in itself, in the process of blooming and fusing with the Central Source. During this process the Inner Fire radiates out with greater and greater magnitude and creates cultures, civilizations, and "objects" of highest beauty.

Beauty is expressed on many levels according to the level on which a Spark is conscious. These are the following levels of beauty:

1. Physical level beauty
2. Emotional level beauty
3. Mental level beauty
4. Intuitional level beauty, and even higher.

The expression of a rare beauty starts when a person's consciousness functions on the intuitional and higher planes where he goes through a process of transfiguration.

Each creativity is charged with the electrical substance through which creative energy of the Inner Core passes. Each beauty presents a different charge.

There is real beauty, and there is artificial beauty. Artificial beauty is a form of beauty the same as the genuine beauty, but it lacks the charge of the higher levels, and it is not based on individual transformation or realization.

Beauty is the manifestation of Divinity within you. The whole creation—our earth and all kingdoms, our solar system, our galaxy, the zodiac and millions of constellations and galaxies—are the manifestation of a consciousness, of a mind, of a power, the Spark

19

of which lives and functions in all forms. And we are, each of us, a Spark of that Central Fire of power.

When we become creative, that Spark begins to manifest. It is the manifestation of that Spark that built the pyramids of the world, and created the art masterpieces in different fields all over the world. The Spark caused the achievements of man in all fields, and created great planetary heroes. The appreciation of beauty is a contact with that Inner Divinity.

Beauty can be discussed from the point of view of the following five types of people:

1. Those fiery artists who are creating beauty. Beauty is the sign of their achievement, realization, and maturity. These are original creators who create in the fiery triangle.

2. Those who strive towards beauty. As they touch, taste, and assimilate beauty their consciousness expands and they enter into the path of creativity.

3. Those who reject beauty due to their immaturity. They are the people upon whom no beauty must be forced, except for the discipline of life, which must be presented in various forms. For once beauty is forced upon them, they turn against it, and against its creators.

4. Those who produce ugliness to oppose beauty. They do this either in full consciousness or mechanically, using the tendency of the majority of people to become excited by crimes and by acts of defaming virtues or heroic actions.

Because of this excitement their ugly productions pay off financially. This does not mean that average humanity has an inclination toward ugliness. On the contrary, average humanity accepts beauty if it is given in a form that it can understand and use. But producers of ugliness have their scientific way of baiting people and through an artificial beauty lead the average person to ugliness. It is surprising how a person can digest ugliness when it is mixed with the right dosage of artificial beauty; one then unconsciously works under the effect of that ugliness. Ugliness can express itself in the form of emotions, in thoughts, in motives, in plans, and in actions. Ugliness conceals the Divinity within, and eventually makes it very hard or very painful for the Divinity to express itself.

Ugliness draws the focus of consciousness to blind drives and urges, toward matter, where it obeys the commands of matter, and of the urges of the physical body. It draws one to the jungle of negative emotions, separative desires, hatred, and crime. Ugliness draws you into your lower mind where fear exists, where illusion exists, where confusion exists. There you lose your life's purpose and wander in the darkness of selfishness.

Those who use beauty to exploit people provide a dangerous trap for those souls who, because of their love of beauty, are trapped and led to the path of ugliness.

The misuse of beauty is the cause of degeneration of cultures, races, and nations. You can find examples of such exploitation in advertisements of sex, tobacco, liquor, in night clubs, in houses of prostitution, in television programs, movies, etc.

The creative spirit cannot change the world until its works are appreciated, accepted and worked on.

Real beauty is conceived in the Spiritual Triad, or in the Triad of Fire:

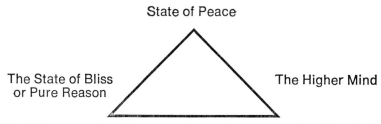

State of Peace

The State of Bliss
or Pure Reason

The Higher Mind

The higher mind is the area where the universal and individual meet, to inspire the individual by the universal.

These three areas when related create a fiery field in which the human soul unfolds into his Divinity. Such a person is called an Agni Yogi, a person who strives for unity in the sphere of fire with cosmic realities. It is in this fiery sphere that the fiery discipline of unity builds its higher vehicles. When we say that man has "higher vehicles," we mean that man is in possession of those subtle mechanisms which are able to convey to him things going on in different levels.

Beauty varies in different areas of life. There is physical beauty, and there is moral beauty. There is beauty of thought and vision. There is beauty of intuition and revelation of mysteries. There is objective beauty and there is subjective beauty. Objective beauty is a condensation and crystallization of subjective beauty. In physical beauty we have only a fraction of real subjective beauty, as in the representation of a glorious palace of sublime architecture when compared with a clay model.

To reach subjective and higher counterparts of beauty one needs "electronic tubes," senses, centers, and higher mechanisms which put the individual self in touch with the higher planes. Such senses and centers are developed in the area of the Spiritual Triad, in the Triangle of Fire.

It is in the Fiery Triangle that man can contact rare beauty in its many forms. All great achievements were born in the Fiery Triangle, because it is there that man can have a vision of the projections coming from Higher realms.

When beauty is conceived in this fiery area it carries with it fire, and sets aflame the Spirit of people with that same fire, and challenges them to a life of beauty.

Man must be gradually initiated into beauty, for beauty exists only when man develops senses to recognize and appreciate beauty.

The imposition of beauty may create many undesirable reactions. Forced beauty irritates those who have no mechanism to receive, assimilate, or express it. This irritation turns into fear and hatred. Persecution of great Masters of Wisdom and of the Arts and Knowledge, originates from such facts.

Once a genius surpasses the levels of consciousness of a large percentage of humanity, his physical destiny is in danger. His art or wisdom is subject to degeneration, serving as food for destructive ugliness, imitations, and distortions.

That is why the sense of beauty must be cultivated from an early age, gradually, and with great watchfulness so that the spirit of beauty is rooted and properly nourished in the hearts of the children of the world.

An imposed dosage of beauty creates rejection toward beauty, or the energy of beauty creates congestions in those who have no way to assimilate and express it.

The charge of beauty must be expressed in creative living, or else it may cause deterioration. You can see this in the history of humanity. Civilizations and cultures created by great Masters of Art and Science, when forced on an unprepared succeeding generation, produce the reverse effect. Degeneration starts after a great achievement of beauty. The reason for this is that the forced voltage of such an achievement was so great that the incoming children were not able to understand, assimilate, and express it. The generation that created such a culture took that beauty for granted and did not prepare the children to appreciate it and to further develop it.

When beauty is forced upon those who are not ready to appreciate and live it creatively, the civilizations enter into a cycle of decay, degeneration, confusion, and chaos.

When degeneration and decay of beauty starts it causes great pain and suffering to those who were identified with its manifold expressions, and they go through a psychological depression. Those who are not yet awake to beauty fall into ugliness, and support the producers of ugliness.

But those initiated souls who were trained in beauty, and were elevated in their consciousness to the great heights of fire, start again to build a new structure of beauty as the testimony of the progress of Spirit throughout the ages. And the wheel turns again and again until man is ready to live in the Fiery Triangle.

A creator is a true artist, is a transmitter who deepens his roots heavenward into as many planes as possible and extends his branches earthward to all it can reach. The purpose is to integrate the lowest with the highest. A transmitter is a conscious bridge, in an unconscious unity.

To appreciate beauty one must build or construct the mechanisms of transmitting centers within himself. Before this mechanism is built, the revelation of great beauties will create suspension of consciousness, total confusion, a sense of purposelessness of life, and destruction of the sense of direction and discrimination.

Do we mean by all this that the great artists must create their masterpieces and not present them to the public? The answer is no. Creative people are always active and their works must be found everywhere. The minority that will respond to their works will elevate themselves to greater spiritual, moral, and cultural achievements.

Those who distort beauty are also active. Those who produce ugliness are very busy with their tasks. And those who are the children of the future have the vision of beauty and are those who will repeatedly bring a new culture and a new beauty in each civilization, until beauty transforms the planetary life.

Let us see what beauty does to those who are open and ready for it: BEAUTY

1. Expands the consciousness.
2. Inspires new visions.
3. Harmonizes unrelated ideas in the mind.
4. Brings new revelations.
5. Releases psychic energy.
6. Evokes joy and love and dispels fear.
7. Makes a man inclusive.
8. Opens the gates of generosity.
9. Awakens greater tolerance.
10. Fills us with solemnity.
11. Regulates the circulation of blood.
12. Regenerates the secretion of glands.
13. Improves the assimilation of food.
14. Creates right human relations.
15. Increases goodwill.
16. Reveals the sense of Infinity and Immortality.

1. Beauty expands the consciousness.

The clarity, intensity, and the depth of your consciousness depends on the quality of the substance of your mental body, and on the source of the ray of intelligence. This ray can come to your mental plane from the human soul, from the Solar Angel, from the Spiritual Triad, or from the Monad itself. The intensity of the light of consciousness increases as the beam of intelligence acts from the centers closer to the true Self.

Also, the consciousness can be focussed onto different levels. If your consciousness is occupied with your physical life or physical body with its urges and drives, and has a certain degree of light, this light will increase more as the focus of your consciousness travels towards the higher planes. If your consciousness is focussed on the higher mental planes without losing its control on lower planes, you have a more balanced consciousness.

When you enjoy beauty in any form, radiated from higher planes, it evokes responses from corresponding planes of your being. Then you begin to feel the inflow of energy coming from that higher plane to the present field of your consciousness. The joy, the frequency, the substance that is released from your higher planes enriches and expands your consciousness, releases it from its lower focus and anchors it on a higher level.

Whenever you taste, enjoy, and fuse with beauty your Inner Core releases a beam of light, a beam of love, and a flow of energy which anchor themselves in the level of your present field of consciousness; thus linking your consciousness with the higher planes of your existence and allowing your consciousness to reach greater horizons and have greater communication with better values.

Thus beauty brings to your consciousness new nourishment: the nourishment of meaning behind the beauty; the nourishment of the creative level in which the artists conceived that beauty; the nourishment of vision, bliss, and labor in which that beauty was galvanized. All this nourishes your consciousness and leads your consciousness toward the plane of intuition, through the symbolism that the beauty represents.

The power of beauty is based on the fact that it is a symbol of a greater joy, bliss, creativity, and vision with which the artist made a contact. When that symbol is contemplated, the power of beauty penetrates into our being and evokes an urge toward beauty.

The task of an artist is to give birth to a new humanity through expanding the vision of humanity to the levels of harmony—to the levels of beauty. An artist conceives new ideas, new ideals, and through them expands the consciousness of humanity. It is through such an expansion that cleavages are healed, new fields of cooperation and understanding are reached, new energies are brought down for daily use, and new visions are presented for human striving.

The practical side of these ideas is that through bringing beauty to one's home, to one's work, and to one's life the consciousness of those who otherwise pursue a life of darkness, ignorance, and separatism is expanded.

A stagnated consciousness cannot be creative. Creativity is the result of an ever expanding consciousness.

2. *Beauty inspires new visions.*

A vision is a fragment of the plan of your Soul which is going to come into actualization in due time. A vision is a portion of the hierarchical Plan which in due time will create response in humanity and turn into reality. Music, writing, dance, sculpture, any kind of creative art bring with it a portion of the plan reflected on the level where the creative act started or where it was conceived.

When you contact the plan behind art, and raise your consciousness, at least temporarily, a part of that plan reflects in your consciousness and you become aware of a new dimension of life, a new vision. This vision changes your life and your relationship and polarizes your life toward the future.

The "future" in its abstract meaning is: the vision that the Solar Life has for the human souls. The future is a magnet which creates response from humanity. The future is the photographic "negative" which will manifest in the form of a picture as a form of life. You can come in contact with higher and more inclusive visions as you raise you consciousness from lower to higher levels.

Let us remember that creativity is twofold: one may be called reflected creativity; the other one, creativity of beingness, or creativity of realization.

The first type of creativity occurs when the artist can reflect the creative works of others, putting them together and producing a new combination of colors, forms, movements, ideas and so on, but he is not in his creation; his creation is not a pouring out of his Self.

The creativity of beingness occurs when the artist is in his creative expression; he is fused with it; he is one with it. In a sense he is his creation. For example, imagine hearing two artists playing violins. One can factually play the given notes, the other one puts his Self into it. You feel the impact of the second one upon your being. When you play your note on the level it was conceived and created, you are a true artist.

True creativity must carry a portion of your being with it. This is the art that impresses people and causes changes in them.

Another example: someone says he loves you, but you do not feel it. But when another one says, "I love you," you feel it and respond to it because it is coming from his beingness, not from the machinery of his being.

A true artist does not come into existence through the process of practice alone. Practice can refine his technique, his style, the ways of his expressions, but he can never be a true artist by just practicing. A true artist comes into being by continuously raising, changing and expanding his consciousness, transforming his life, and penetrating into the higher levels of his being in an ever-inclusive spirit. Often such an artist does not even need to learn the contemporary rules and regulations of expression. His Inner fullness pours out and shines in rare beauty and in a rare and unprecedented technique and form, because beauty is the Self. Art is the manifestation of Self in ever-expanding inclusiveness.

Sometimes we discriminate between different types of music. We say, "This type of music is good; that music is not good." But the reality is that some music is conceived and created while the focus of consciousness of the artist was in the intuitional or higher planes, and some music was created while the consciousness of man was focussed in the sacral or solar plexus center.

Those people who are focussed in their lower levels will not like the music coming from the higher levels. And those people who are focussed on higher levels will be hurt when subjected to lower level music. They will degenerate, or at least they will be confused.

Real beauty is a presentation of a high level, which like a magnet, pulls up those who are ready for it, or gradually makes them ready to be uplifted.

3. *Beauty harmonizes unrelated ideas in the mind.*

Ideas are fragments of the Plan dropped into our mental pool through our visions, prayers, and meditation. But because they are not aligned and integrated as a whole, they do not present a power and influence in our life and do not come into expression as a creative act. Beauty brings these ideas together and presents to them a goal for existence and an urge to express themselves collectively.

It is as a man who comes to a bazaar and finds ten to fifteen boys lying down there and wasting their time in arguments. He approaches them and says, "I have a garden to plant; if you want to make some money, follow me."

They all join him and work cooperatively on one goal. They may be antagonistic toward each other, but when a goal is presented to them, they become cooperative and united.

Each beauty is a melody, or a symphony, of ideas. When it comes, its impact on the human mind is just like a magnet which aligns and integrates, and creates a goal for the tiny pieces of metal in the field.

Beauty creates goals in us, gives a meaning to our life, and around this goal or meaning our chaotic mind eventually organizes itself. An organized mind is a power source. A disorganized mind causes leakage of energy.

There are many beautiful ideas in our minds, but because of lack of links between them, they are powerless and static. Beauty forges the link between them, and when they fuse with each other the creativity of man becomes active.

Those people who have a harmonized mind can be recognized immediately. When you discuss anything with them, they help put your mind into orderly action. They dispel your uncertainty or confusion, and give you a clear outlook on life.

Creators of beauty are the co-workers of the Great Power in the Cosmos.

4. *Beauty brings new revelations.*

A revelation is the result of the ability to see things that you never saw before although they were there. A veil drops from your eyes and you say, "I see now."

A beauty is the result of a revelation. Revelation is nothing else but a moment of penetration into the veil of the mystery of your Being, or of the Universe.

The created beauty, being thus a messenger of revelation, brings to you a new reality of which previously you were unaware. This revelation creates a new polarization in your life and you begin to organize your psychological and physical life according to the revelation.

Revelation is an experience resulting from the interaction of two poles of being. It is the result of removing the veils of your personality and allowing the eye to see things free from the limitations of the personality. It is also the result of the withdrawal of the human soul into the Source of being, the Self. Thus veil after veil and stage after stage, man is awakened to reality; every stage of awakening is a new act of revelation.

First you relate yourself to the world from the interests of your physical instruments, urges and drives, and handle life for the sake of your physical existence. Then that veil drops down and you see a greater meaning in a life of larger relationships, subtler feelings, and you relate yourself to the world emotionally. There is pain and pleasure. There is sorrow and joy, not for yourself only, but for those who are closely related to you.

Then the next veil drops, the veil of the lower mind full of illusions, and you relate yourself to the world as a mind. The world for you now is law and order, mathematics, geometry, algebra, design, and plan. If you are fortunate, that veil also drops, and you touch the existence as it is on the intuitional plane. Thus veil after veil drops and your vision penetrates deeper into the mystery of life.

This is a process of awakening. As you awaken more you are more aware, until the awareness unit itself is the object of awareness. Thus the greatest revelation starts when your eyes begin to see your true Self, first as in a mirror, then "face to face."

Initiation is the process of the removal of the veils from your consciousness, and later from your awareness.

As you awaken, you go to your true Self. As you go toward matter you go into a deeper and deeper sleep, and into separation and crystallization.

It is the beauty projected from deeper layers of a truly creative artist that leads your steps to the sanctuary of your own being as you enjoy and worship the beauty he created and are thrilled by it.

You cannot really enjoy beauty unless you are one with beauty. That is what the adornment of beauty is. Until you are lost in beauty you cannot adorn beauty. In adornment the separative considerations are annihilated. That is one of the secrets of the great arts—to annihilate your considerations based on the separated self.

One day a mystic said that he entered into the garden of beauty and lost his self. When he came back to his friends they asked, "What did you bring from the garden of beauty?" He answered "Beauty," because he was transformed into beauty.

5. Beauty releases psychic energy.

Psychic energy is the energy flow which comes out of your Innermost Center, out of your creative Core, electrifying and charging all your vehicles with the energy of life, love, and light. It is the energy that brings to your vehicles the harmony, the bliss and the serenity of the Inner Self. When psychic energy circulates freely in the personality vehicles, it harmonizes man with the rhythm of the Cosmic Life.

Great artists and leaders have a greater charge of psychic energy which radiates out of them: deeds, words, thoughts, and creative expressions. This psychic energy gives fiery quality to your expressions, and whatever you do you put people in enthusiastic action.

Beauty releases psychic energy because beauty causes the Innermost Divinity to manifest. It evokes the Divinity in you, makes your Divinity radioactive. When the radioactivity of beauty starts you are in a process of healing. This energy purifies your threefold vehicles and restores harmony and health in them.

It is beauty that unifies and integrates all those vehicles with the central rhythm of the Self. Those who become one with their true Self become the embodiments of beauty.

Once I was trying to find the most glorious beauty when the name of Christ flashed into my mind. The embodiment of beauty is the One Who was and still is demonstrating the greatest love not only for His friends but also for His enemies. This is not all. He was and still is demonstrating a life, which if really adopted, will lead the whole human race to the summit of beauty. He is the path of psychic energy. That is why He said, "I am the path, the truth and the life." And He synthesized the great idea and vision saying, "I am the wine, drink it. I am the bread, eat it . . ." Thus one can be fused with Sublime Beauty.

It is psychic energy that carries out the influences, the impression of your purpose and plan, and the Inner Fire. Nothing is positively influenced unless it is charged by psychic energy. Your voice, your speech, your music, your paintings, all are mechanical and evoke only a transient response if not charged with psychic energy.

When you have a flow of psychic energy you *touch* people, you touch their Essence, their heart. They are touched not through your words or any expressions, but by *your Self*.

Man is a unit of energy, a wave of electricity which radiates and nourishes all the little lives of his vehicles. Similarly, expression charged with psychic energy nourishes all those who come in contact with that expression in any form, and this contact creates in them temporary or perpetual self-realization.

Man in his Essence is a flame, a living fire, and this fire burns in his creative expression.

Imagine a chalice in which there is a flame and you are serving the flame as a holy communion; that flame is the psychic energy.

6. *Beauty evokes joy and love and dispels fear.*

Ancient kings of China and Mongolia knew this. They decorated their palaces with rare beauties. They had music, dances, sculpture, high level literature and highly refined needlework. They had all this because they knew that leadership cannot move in the right direction unless the leader has joy and love.

Joy comes from artfully transcending personality limitations and directing the consciousness to a level where you have everything, you lose nothing, and you *are.*

Love comes from the level where you feel one with all life. When you are able to shatter the limitations of your physical, emotional, and mental conditions and enter into the freedom of your spirit, you are in joy. When love releases itself in our being and floods our whole life, fear is overcome and unity is established.

Beauty releases a person from his limitation and carries him to the Source of unity.

Lies and exploitations limit us. Truth and service make us free. That is why we feel joy in freedom, and love in unity.

7. *Beauty makes a man inclusive.*

The greatest remedy for selfish, separative, and hateful people is beauty coming from Higher Sources. This beauty must be given to them as seed-thoughts for meditation, like pills for assimilation.

Beauty transcends all separations. In front of beauty there is no racial discrimination, no exploitation, no aggressive selfishness. Beauty unites all men everywhere, because beauty is the language of unity. In beauty we mean not only political unity, but unity of emotions, unity of mind, unity of Souls, unity of responses.

As we adore beauty we fuse with beauty, and our heart opens to all living beings.

8. *Beauty opens the gates of generosity.*

When you see a beautiful woman or a beautiful man you want to give gifts, because his or her beauty makes you act as a Soul, not as a personality.

Those who are stingy are matter-bound, personality and fear-bound. Raise their consciousness to Soul level, and they will become giving persons.

As you go higher in your being you become more radioactive; as you go down, you become more respressive. To be repressed means to be non-radioactive, to shrink, to withdraw into your pitiful lower self and its interests. Economy is not repression or stinginess, but the right appropriation of energy for the need.

9. *Beauty awakens greater tolerance.*

Beauty widens your consciousness and makes you know that in each person there is "the hope of glory" which will one day manifest itself.

Tolerance is the ability to see motives, and the conviction that wrong motives are like meteors which shine for awhile, but eventually die in space.

Beauty increases the power of your intuition because it links your mind and your emotions with the plane of intuition. Intuition stands in relation to the mind as the father stands in relation to his child who is playing with his toys.

No real beauty comes into being without the fire of intuition or the fire of inclusive vision.

10. *Beauty fills us with solemnity.*

Solemnity is the result of alignment with the Inner Creative Center. Solemnity is experienced when you enjoy beauty on its level, grasp its message and radiate it out.

Beauty inspires a man to strive towards his destiny. It opens in him a way to the understanding of the purpose of life. Beauty opens you to the grandeur of existence.

Solemnity is the realization that a man is one with the creative Source and beauty.

Solemnity does not scatter the pearls of wisdom and beauty in the bazaars. Imposed beauty degenerates people and turns them against beauty.

Solemnity gradually reveals beauty as people grow in their consciousness and appreciate and strive toward it.

Exposure to too much beauty may blind people. That is why rare beauties of ceremonies, rituals, and wisdom were conveyed only in inner sanctuaries.

Solemnity and simplicity appropriate the fire of beauty to the level of life. Whenever solemnity is lacking beauty disappears.

11. *Beauty regulates the circulation of blood.*

The heart specialists will be surprised when they investigate this subject. Irregularity of blood circulation and irregularity of heartbeat are the direct or indirect results of chaotic emotions, contradictory post hypnotic suggestions, and unrelated opposing and conflicting thoughtforms.

Beauty creates a symphony in the mental and emotional planes, and gradually clears away the post hypnotic suggestions as the man raises his consciousness from the lower mental plane to the higher mental plane.

12. *Beauty regenerates the secretion of the glands.*

The secretion of the glands depends on the etheric centers which mainly condition the seven ductless glands.

Beauty brings psychic energy into the center of each chakra, and nourishes and regulates them with the key to the inner plan and the inner purpose. The keynote of the human being is the plan. Beauty brings that key to the centers through the psychic energy which it releases.

You emit fragrance when you enjoy beauty. You emit an unpleasant odor when your mind and emotions are occupied with ugliness and crimes.

13. *Beauty improves the assimilation of food.*

That is why kings who were initiates used to eat in the most beautiful environment with music, dance, color, and form.

Beauty creates synchronization of the organs, glands and centers and helps to expel their poison as one perspires.

Those who have indigestion are under the pressure of ugly conditions. Change the conditions and the digestion will improve.

14. *Beauty creates right human relations.*

The greatest friendship is friendship in beauty. Friendship in beauty never fades away but increases and becomes luminous. A right human relation is having respect for the existence of Divinity in each human being.

15. *Beauty increases goodwill.*

Goodwill is our intensive urge to protect and to nourish the life of each Divine Spark in manifestation.

It is also true that beauty and goodwill reveal ugliness and cleavages. You are never aware of the ugliness going on around you until you have seen beauty. You never realize that so much ill-will is in existence in the world until you begin to live a life based on goodwill. But the miracle is that after you see ugliness and ill-will, you pour out greater love from your heart, and try to reach the Inner Divinity even in those who are aberrated and intoxicated by ugliness and crimes.

16. *Beauty reveals the sense of Infinity and Immortality.*

At the time you deeply enjoy a real beauty you transcend time and matter, and your consciousness enters a state of timelessness.

Immortality is sensed immediately when your Soul eliminates the prisons of your physical, emotional, and mental limitations. Through beauty you get closer to the Innermost Self within you and others, that Self which is the door towards Immortality and Infinity.

Beauty is beingness; it is a process of transformation and transfiguration. Beauty is the objectification of divinity. It is the charcoal turning into fire. There is no beauty without living that beauty. Great artists do not reflect beauty; they are the beauty. The beauty when reflected, loses its charge. Beauty objectified in life carries a tremendous charge. No one can be a great artist and creator of beauty until he becomes the beauty itself, becomes one with his Inner Divinity, in all his relations with life.

One cannot enjoy beauty and express ugliness without endangering his life. Such a condition creates great psychological disturbances in man with dire physical effects.

The suffering of an artist is greater when he releases a charge of great beauty and psychic energy, and this charge is resisted by the glamors, illusions, and maya of people still wandering in the lower levels. The two clash and there is great turmoil in the life of the artist.

The germs of negativity act violently when an artist releases higher energies into his system. Also due to his sensitivity, he absorbs the ills of his environment and identifies with them, again creating chaos in his system. In addition, due to his alignment and integration, any pressure on any of his vehicles spreads all over his personality, and he suffers intensely.

Once an artist recreates himself or has an experience of a new birth in which all his personality vehicles stand as a beauty of the transfigured Self, his suffering ends. From then on he creates in bliss. These are the genuises who function in the Spiritual Triad, and their artwork is their *own life*.

M.M., in speaking about beauty says,

"The miracle of Beauty in the adornment of our daily lives will exalt mankind."[3]

"Uphold Thy Light.
Illumine the beauties of My Temple.
Teach the Joy of Beauty."[4]

"Christ's deeds were consummated amidst the beauties of nature. Never did He dwell for long in cities."[5]

"We have determined to reveal the ways of enlightening cruel hearts to soften them by the balm of Beauty."[6]

"A pure conception of music helps the transmission of the current.
We pray by sounds and by the symbols of Beauty."[7]

"The character of the people will be illumined by the **beauty of spirit**."[8]

"It is better to know men than to be deceived by their masks."[9]

"If human hearts were filled with beauty, no sacrifices would be needed.
But manifold are the dark ones.
Therefore, it is a thorny way that leads to each truth."[10]

"Yes, Yes, Yes, each word of unity is as the seed of some fair flower."[11]

"Repeat Beauty again and again, even with tears, until you reach your destiny."[12]

"To cultivate a garden of beauty is permitted to all."[13]

"Blessed are you who aspire to Beauty."[14]

BEAUTY

IV

BEAUTY MAKES OUR PERSONALITY strive towards the spiritual path because beauty stimulates the Spirit aspect of man, and the Spirit creates polarization in personality.

Beauty evokes striving. Man sees his own true nature when surrounded with beauty. Beauty is one of the avenues to self-knowledge.

It is futile sometimes to criticize or advise people to change their ways of life, as long as they do not have something to compare themselves with they are satisfied with what they are. When a beauty catches their eye, or their spirit, the real change starts in their nature.

I often think that women have a tremendous influence upon man, not because of their sex, but because of their sense of beauty. Throughout history women worshipped those men who presented a vision of beauty for them.

Children especially unfold through beauty. If we surround children with beauty: the beauty of words, color, sound, form, and movement we will not have increasing crimes.

Beauty puts the strings of their harp in tune, and the impressions coming from Higher and Solar Sources instead of creating noise will create music and harmony in them. Man reacts according to how he is built, and by what substance his vehicles are built.

Those who strive towards beauty, gradually live a goal-fitting life. They adjust and harmonize their actions on all levels to make them reach the goal.

The moments of beauty are the moments of the revelation of our goals. Beauty tunes in our mind with the Inner Guide who knows our goal.

Worship was and is a technique to create polarization, striving, goal-fitness; but beyond that, worship is a means through which man becomes that which he worships.

The stories of powerful, omnipresent, omniscient, and creative Gods were the main incentive of the progress and striving of many races.

Give a vision to people and they will improve their life. Thus worship of beauty imposes a process of purification in our nature. Man begins to change his physical life, his emotional reactions or responses, his mental attitudes, viewpoints, and thoughts. Thus an overall change can be induced within our nature through worship of beauty.

This is a way of mastery over our nature. Give children objects of worship and they will organize their life to obtain that object, or to be the object itself.

Worship is considered an emotional or devotional attitude. But it is something beyond that. In worship the man in one part of his nature intuitively feels that he is one with the object, but in the reflective part of his nature he wants to be that object. In worship this separated part of his self comes to an at-one-ment.

Beauty awakens in us the feeling of gratitude. This is a very interesting point. Real gratitude is the feeling that one already is a beauty. He is essentially a beauty and he lives in beauty because all creation is beautiful. Such a realization of being a part of that beauty is gratitude.

Gratitude is not a feeling of thinking only, but is a realization of beingness. As you become aware of the beauty of creation and of the beauty of your own existence, the spirit of gratitude deepens in your heart. Gratitude dawns in our hearts as soon as we experience beauty in any form.

Beauty thus creates unity and the deepest sense of love. Love is a state of consciousness of unity, which is not affected by our physical, emotional, and mental reactions. Once you are above these reactions you truly love. You have unconditional love.

Beauty takes you above your limited self-interest and challenges you to have such interests which are related to the greatest number of people. Self-interest is a level of consciousness in which man is limited with his physical, emotional, and mental need. He has a wall around himself, and he thinks that the most important being existing in the world, is himself. But once he sees a beauty, and begins to strive towards that beauty, he slowly comes out of his self-made prison, and experiences a new world, in which he is not the center, but the part of a great configuration.

This is how generosity starts in a man. Ownership makes a man greedy. Once a man sees that he does not own anything he becomes generous. He sees that nature offers itself free. Only man makes business with nature. Ownership is a mental attitude, not a state of having possessions.

Think about the sun, think about the air, the ocean, the rivers, the forests, the rain, the rainbow, flowers; all is for all. How can one see beauty and still live in a consciousness of greed. Beauty makes us realize that nature is all giving. A greedy man lives for himself; a generous man lives for others.

Beauty leads us into Self-actualization. Self-actualization is the process of enlightenment during which you find your own Self in the Self of others, and eventually become one with the Self in everything. That was the message of Krishna and Christ. In becoming Oneself, you become all-giving, all-loving. Real Self-actualized persons such as Buddha, Krishna, Christ, Zoroaster and others, were all-loving and all-giving. That is how a true server of the race emerges. The degree of your service is the degree of your self-forgetfulness.

Self-forgetfulness is not forgetting your essential Self, but is an act of leaving behind the interferences of your false self, of your glamors, illusions, and their urges and drives which act as if they were the Self.

In creating beauty we forget ourselves. The most self-forgetful people are those servers of the race who give a new birth to the racial consciousness, or create those art-works which transform the life.

We sometimes limit beauty to the field of art, but real beauty can express itself in any avenue of life. It can express itself in politics, in education, in human relationships and communications, or in philosophy. It can express itself in science, in religion, in ceremony, even finance.

One day a person asked me if a politician can create beauty. I said that the real meaning of politics is to establish those laws and principles which will serve the cause of the highest good of the planet, and put them in action.

Politics is the process of tuning in the human will with the Plan and Purpose of the Great Life, the body of which is this planet, with humanity as one of its organs.

What a great beauty can be created in the synthesis of all religions and in actualization of the principles of that synthesis. Religions brought such an abundanc of beauty in music, vestments, vessels, ceremonies, architecture, and sculpture.

Education is a great avenue to express beauty, because in true education the person is put in contact with his transpersonal Self.

There is a great beauty developing in the methods of finance and economy. Our international banking system, our financial techniques are quite beautiful, but will be more so in the future when in all of the systems everyone will be dedicated to the service of mankind.

Thus the Self, which is in every living form, will come into manifestation through beauty.

All great Souls were the embodiments of beauty in a certain degree. Krishna was a great beauty. Buddha was a great beauty. Christ was a great beauty. Their disciples were shining beauties for all ages.

In all ages, those who uplifted human life were beautiful not only physically, but also in their words, relationships, thoughts, and works.

I remember talking with a musician, saying that there are some exceptionally beautiful passages in the New Testament. He laughed and said, "Show me one." I opened the New Testament and said, "Read here."

'Father forgive them, as they do not know what they are doing.'[15]

Then to see the idea more clearly he read a few verses before and after that verse. As he read his face became very serious and drops of tears came to his eyes. Finally he said, "If I could only create a music which could express the depth of the beauty of this moment, I would be able to express my gratitude to Him."

What was the beauty he saw? Was it a vision or revelation or greatness that was hard to crush? I never saw my friend again. He sold all his possessions and disappeared.

The beauty he saw was so strong that it caused a major change in his life. Such changes occur in our life through meditation on a great beauty. Meditation leads you into beauty, and makes all your expressions beautiful.

Thinking may not do the same thing. The difference between meditation and thinking can be explained thus:

In meditation your physical, emotional, and mental activities are tuned in with the plan of the Inner Light, and they are under training to manifest the Inner Light in all their endeavors.

In thinking, this alignment is not yet present. The mind is used for physical, emotional, or mental purposes with separative interests. But once the mind is used by the unfolding human soul in harmony with the Light of the Inner Guide, the thinking changes into meditation. Meditation is a process of thinking inspired by the motive of the Inner Guide.

Through thinking you can find the same principles or laws of the nature, as you do in meditation. But you can use these principles and laws for your separative goals, or destructive and selfish goals.

In meditation, all the principles and laws are used in harmony with the Plan and for the benefit of all humanity, or they are used for the survival of all life and for the expression of beauty.

On the road of beauty the fragrance of respect radiates out of our beauty. The fountainhead of respect is beauty. Only beauty inspires respect.

Beauty in oneself, beauty in others, draws people closer and reveals the Essential Divinity in them.

Respectfulness is the recognition of the divinity in gratitude. In ancient times very strong emphasis was laid upon respect. All relationships of high level contacts should be based upon respectful manners, words, and even thoughts. Thus the ancients recognized one of the paths leading to Hierarchy.

Mutual respect creates electrical discharges between the persons involved. In mutual respect we have a shifting of polarities. For example, as soon as you respect someone your frequency is raised to a higher level. Conversely, the frequency of the other persons is raised at the time they recognize or affirm your act of respect. Thus, respect changes the polarization of people and raises their level of frequency.

He who offers respect starts a positive charge. The one who received has a receptive polarity, but immediately when he acknowledges the current of respect, it changes into positive polarity and passes the current of energy, amplified by his thought, to the person who respected him, who then changes his polarity into receptivity. And this polarity systematically is altered often, until again, one's polarity prevails between the persons, or a continuous flow is established between the admirer and the object of admiration. This is how psychic energy circulates within many individual and group relationships.

One does not need to touch the object of respect to express energy exchange. The moment of true respect is the moment when psychic energy is in action.

Any act of respect, which is contaminated with doubt, expectations, critical thoughts, vanity, jealousy, insincerity, mechanicalness of the act—creates short circuits, and the exchange of psychic energy is absent. In many cases the seeds of animosity are planted when the respect is forced, or based on expectations, or rendered in an insincere attitude.

It is only in the spirit of respect that the parent's blessings pass to their children, the Teacher's wisdom is transmitted to his disciples, and the commands of the leaders are understood by the warriors. The currents established by mutual respect serve eventually as the carrier of telepathic communication.

Thus respect bridges the gaps, creates synthesis, and leads to Hierarchy.

The act of respect is the recognition of Divinity in the person, no matter in what degree that divinity is in expression. Hence, respect is the moment of contact of the Divine Spark. That is why in every act of respect there is pleasure, there is joy, there is bliss. Pleasure, joy, and bliss are the effects of the exchange of psychic energy. As one goes deeper in his respectfulness, the sensations are more inclusive and purer. To teach the children of the race the science of beauty and respect, initiates gave thoughtfully prepared manners, such as prostration, bowing, putting your right hand on your heart, sitting before the knees of the Teacher, keeping a space behind when walking with the Teacher, standing at the moment of his entrance, sitting after he is seated, using special phrases to amplify your respect, conscious consideration and obedience to his guidance or hints.

But all these manners, words, and signs become outworn shells when the true spirit of respectfulness vanishes, and turns into mechanical expressions.

It is the time to bring out the true spirit of respect at the close approach of the externalization of the Hierarchy. No higher value can penetrate into your consciousness except through receptivity created by respect.

Beauty can be used to:

1. Transform lives of people.
2. To create efficiency in office work and in general labor carried on in any department of service.
3. To create goals within the minds of students in various levels.
4. To create striving towards betterment in life.
5. To create the sense of responsibility.
6. To create respect for any form of life.
7. To raise the consciousness to higher values.
8. To create better health in physical, emotional, and mental levels.
9. To create right human relations and goodwill.
10. To create understanding and harmlessness.
11. To help people see the life from higher, broader, and all-inclusive dimensions.
12. To create telepathic communications.
13. To create sensitivity for higher impressions.
14. To stimulate the power of creativity.
15. To inspire the spirit of gratitude.

There is not a phase of human life which cannot be improved by the power of beauty.

To begin with, let us take as an example a youth rehabilitation center. The goal of a rehabilitation center is to inspire the inhabitants to recognize and appreciate the values of

—time
—prosperity
—life
—human beings
—and other life forms.

Most of the people that are taken to rehabilitation centers are the violators, in a certain degree, of the rules or laws of our society from legal or moral viewpoints, and if we condense all these rules and laws we can see that they are related to time, property, life, human beings, and to other life forms.

These violators are intentional or unconscious, but there is a common denominator related to violations and that is *ugliness.*

Ugliness is defined as acts or forms which are generally based on:

Selfish motives
Crimes
Separativeness
Hate
Greed
Fear
Distortions
Lies
Jealousy
Waste
Gossip
Inertia
Lack of alignment or integrity
Sickness
Ingratitude
Totalitarian attitudes.

People living in such environments will have a very hard time keeping their integrity and sanity.

The distortions and disturbances take place in the nature of youth between the ages of three and twenty-one years. In these years they resemble a harp with very sensitive strings. Any form of ugliness loosens the strings or intensifies them creating a discord. Gradually the attunement of the whole instrument is distored and the person engages himself with the acts that are against his physical health, his moral integrity, spiritual creativity, and human dignity.

To help such people to a certain degree, the first prerequisite is to create an environment which radiates beauty, beauty in

—form
—color
—sound

—action and movement
—words
—expressions
—ideas
—and visions.

Those who are working in such centers must be graduated from a special school which teaches them:

1. The science of harmony in color, sound, movements, and forms.
2. The science of communication with people in a disciplined voice with a well mastered vocabulary and manners.
3. To see the seeds of beauty in others.
4. How to dress, choosing the right colors, styles that fit for various occasions.
5. How to care but not to be caught in personality networks.
6. How to decorate the rooms, the offices, the halls, the bathroom, and the bedroom to create a spirit of upliftment and harmony.
7. How to be an example of beauty.
8. How to inspire people with the spirit of heroism and service for the common good.

The highest achievement of the human soul is the moment of identification with the principle of beauty. When a certain number of teachers, leaders, and public officials are graduated with the qualifications of beauty, then we will see the dawn of a new life.

When the rehabilitation centers turn into centers of beauty, they will change into schools of creativity; creativity not only in the arts, but creativity in relation to the human nature. They will change into schools in which a man can go and be "reborn" again.

The rehabilitation center's environment: buildings, decoration, and personnel must be a total contrast to the environment from which the distorted youth comes.

They must feel that with their muddy "body," they are entering a clear and clean pool; they are entering into peace, harmony, love, respect; they are entering into a sphere of understanding, discipline, strength, and reality.

It is in this place that they will hear the call of their transpersonal Self. They will sense the hand of beauty tuning the strings of their nature. They will see that the human dignity really exists. They will realize that the institution is not a prison for them but a rare opportunity to meet themselves and to radiate out the best that they have. Graduates from such rehabilitation centers will introduce great changes in the social and cultural life.

They will see that it is possible to have a different world, different than the world in which they used to waste the precious days and years and energies of their life.

The flow of life is forever lost except when it is used to build the future.

In the curriculum of such institutions, a great amount of time must be given to the "appreciation of beauty."

The inhabitants, or better to say the students, will have time to listen to classical music and the inspiring music of choirs of great churches.

It must be noted here that great music, which can transform the life of a man, is the music which is created by highly evolved human beings who were inspired by higher ideas of human dignity, Infinity, heroism, unity, contact with higher forces of nature; by the ideas of beauty, sacrifice, and love; by the ideas of ever-progressive transfiguration of nature, and the resurrection of the human spirit from all limitations.

Such music must be introduced on a gradient scale with the right dosage. Let us remember that beauty is energy and people must be introduced to beauty gradually.

First they must learn to appreciate:

—the beauty of sound, the music of the streams, rivers, waterfalls;
—the music of the wind and the breeze when it is passing through the trees, bushes, and fields;
—the music of the birds at dawn and at sunset;
—the beauty of the human voice and the melodies and symphonies of great masters.

The next step is to introduce students to visual beauty:

—the beauty of colors, movements, forms, relationships or proportions, paintings, and other art works of great artists;

—the beauty of the mountains, forests, rivers, lakes, and oceans—
the sailboat;
—the beauty of the stars.

The next step can be to introduce the beauty of the human
emotions:

—love, all-inclusive love, respect, fearlessness, kindness, peaceful-
ness, enthusiasm, and joy.

All of these can be presented through dramatic performances
with color and music.

Next, the beauty of great ideas can be presented to the students.
Great heroes and great leaders and great geniuses in any field are
those who are inspired by great ideas:

—ideas of freedom;
—ideas of unity;
—ideas of mastery of time, matter, space, human limitations;
—ideas of great service and illumination of the masses;
—ideas of a world without crimes;
—ideas of brotherhood of humanity;
—ideas of life after death.

These ideas can be presented through those historic men and
women who are daring enough to live these ideas and manifest
them through all their relationships.

The student must see the beauty of the true political leaders,
the beauty of true educators and philosophers, the beauty of great
creative people, the beauty of great scientists, the beauty of the true
religion, and the beauty of human sharing which is what true
economy is.

We need a mobilization of beauty, not only in our rehabilitation
centers, but also in our prisons, hospitals, government offices,
courts, streets, and cities.

Beauty releases the divine principles in man.

There will be no success, abundance, joy, health, and progress
unless we act and live not only as physical, emotional, and mental
beings but also as divine principles and divine beauties.

Chapter 2

CREATIVE EFFORTS

HERE ARE MANY MECHANICAL ways to produce objects of art, but they are not the result of creative efforts. Mechanically produced art objects do not carry the energy that brings changes in those who contact the objects.

Creative efforts cause progressive changes in those who are involved in the efforts, and in those who come in contact with the objects of creative efforts.

A true art object, which is produced by creative efforts, evokes efforts toward universality, purity, simplicity, cooperation. It expands the consciousness. It brings changes within the soul of man which enables him to see greater meaning and beauty in life.

Mechanical productivity of art objects is not the goal of art. Art is a self-unfoldment process. It is an effort to bring out the beauty latent in every man.

Once when I was visiting a friend in his home he moved across the room and went to the piano and began to play a very difficult sounding piece. I couldn't believe he played that well because I knew that he never practiced. I walked over to him and saw that a player piano roll was mechanically activating the keys—his playing was purely artificial.

There are machines which can create various designs on materials, on carpets, on wall paper. There are machines which combine colors and produce colorful forms, but such mechanical productions do not create efforts toward progressive perfection.

I had a friend who used to produce hundreds of little statues from moldings. These are forms of art production which lack creative effort.

Art is also used to exploit human beings, to condition them, and to brainwash them for various purposes. Some music is especially produced to stimulate sex or aggressiveness and to block thinking and striving for a better life. The victims of such music act as slaves, and one can exploit their bodies, their sexuality, their finances, and lead them to any imaginable activity and crime.

Truly creative people try to counteract such kinds of exploitation. They try to create greater art objects, and to offset the effects of the pseudo-creativity. Through their arts, greater vision and depth they offer and lead the participant to higher striving and discipline.

Once in a class of esoteric studies, my teacher said that we do not dig trenches to bury our enemies, but we raise mountains to greater heights beside them. This is how creative people can attract the attention of the greater public and help them to develop deeper discrimination. Cheap art grows fast like a weed; real art grows slowly, but in comparison to the weed it becomes an oak tree which lasts centuries with its blessings.

Real creative effort has three labors:

I. The first labor is to reconstruct our physical, emotional, and mental equipment. We must improve our physical body, our manners, the way we dress, walk, and act. We must improve and change the way we feel, react, or respond. We must change the way we use our speech. We must eliminate all conversation that is not goal-fitting, replacing it with conversation that is full of meaning, beauty, and solemnity.

We must change the way we think by eliminating the walls and the mechanical processes in our thinking and make it more creative. We must clear away unworthy thought patterns and habits, and cast away fears and doubts. We must eliminate as much as possible all the seeds of being a show-off, a flatterer, or a gossip.

Show-off or flattery build a false personality, which, later as man advances in knowledge, become a great danger and hindrance. The real Self gets lost under the heavy formation of a false personality, and man becomes a machine to be used by outer forces. Your creativity and survival depends on your Essence. As your false personality grows bigger, your intuitive power, your conscience, and your power of discrimination wane, and the possibility of your survival becomes less and less.

It is important to remember that we build our mechanism through responding to the world from a higher level, and from a new point of view. *It is our responses that build us.* This is such an important statement. As you respond to higher frequencies, greater ideas and visions in greater inclusiveness, you build yourself with finer substance and with better engineering.

When a person meditates, studies, and attends lectures he develops his intellect and accumulates a lot of knowledge, but these do not serve him unless he changes his mechanism through creative expressions, through practical living, through the higher ideas he came in contact with during his creative efforts.

Through practical living and higher creative ideas you change and refine your mechanism and make it more receptive to waves of greater inspiration. The foundation of all art is man himself. Whatever he is, his art is the reflection, even the manifestation, of his Being.

As the consciousness of man expands and he begins to work on higher and higher planes, he channels greater light and wisdom and greater beauty.

Do not be afraid when you do not reach your goal or achieve the level you planned to achieve. But, beware of not striving. The day you give up striving, you are in danger of drowning in a waterfall. The sooner you get rid of the pull of downpouring water, the greater will be your spiritual progress.

II. The second labor is to achieve a level, and try to create from that level, without losing its frequency. It is this new frequency that must express itself through all your creative efforts until you raise it higher.

We know that we have high points daily, weekly or monthly. In these high points we touch some great beauty, we feel great expansion of consciousness, we see new visions, we see the Plan more clearly, we move up to a new step on the ladder of our evolution. But often these high points last only a few seconds, and then we come down to our usual level.

The secret of creativity is the ability to hold that frequency as long as possible and engage yourself in creative labor. Some geniuses were able to stay on the achieved frequency for days, others for months, even years, until their masterpieces were created. Some of them maintained their high level as a base to strive to higher and higher levels.

Such creativity is not coming from your technique, your knowledge, your skill, but is coming from the energy field of a new level into which your consciousness was able to penetrate. However, you are always using your knowledge, your technique and your style in your labor of creativity.

Whenever you come down from your high level to your normal consciousness and try to create, you act from the memory of that high level, but you do not have that same voltage of energy within you. But when you create from the higher level that you were able to reach, you channel the energy of that high level. Eventually you get used to it and that high level becomes your normal level, which you then use as a base to strive toward higher levels.

In creating on higher levels, you transmit through the object of your art the same frequency you are in. Those who come in contact with your art feel the creative wave thus raising them up to a new level of awareness. This is how change occurs in those who come in contact with your higher creative expressions.

Whenever one creates from the high level he reached at the time of his creative labor, he charges his aura with the energy of that level, and causes transformation within his own nature. When a few days or hours later, the artist comes down to his "normal" level, he carries in his aura a lot of the substance from higher realms. This substance enables him to climb there again with less effort and stay there longer, until the time when his aura becomes so saturated with the substance that the high level becomes a normal level for him.

Creativity is a level. As you raise your level of beingness through transformation, transfiguration, and resurrection you come in contact with Greater Lives who are Creative Sources. Their substance, or fire, gives you greater vision and inspiration and causes greater striving.

There are two levels of creativity:

One is to create new decorations, dramatizations, and movement presenting the same great principles and fundamentals.

The next is to create new fundamentals and principles, and present them with new and higher decorations, dramatizations, and movement.

The first can be done when you study and practice but do not change your level. For the second you must change your level.

One can create only that which he is. The life of Christ is a great creative art, because His level of beingness touches Cosmic planes. Such an art creates new civilizations, new visions and greater striving toward perfection. It is not artificial but conscious manifestation of one's own real Self.

The greatest artist is the one who achieves greater heights of unfoldment.

True art can be discriminated from false art by observing its effect on people. If the art creates striving toward improvement and perfection, if the art creates a deeper sense of responsibility and duty, greater love and cooperation, then that art comes from Higher Sources.

If the art increases crime, causes greater attachment to material values and physical pleasures, puts pressure on people to escape from their responsibilities through drugs, alcohol, marijuana and uncontrolled sex, then such art is destructive and self-oriented.

The most important thing in art is the energy transformed by the artist into the object of his art. This transformed energy comes from the level of the artist, or from the level he is in contact with. It is this energy which produces changes in others and opens deeper levels of their beings. If this energy is not there, the object of art has no real value.

A man can give a lecture and be well versed in his subject matter, but his lecture will carry no energy if it is coming from his store of knowledge and not from the level of his spiritual achievement. When there is no spiritual achievement, his lecture or dance, his music or song, comes from his three-fold mechanism, not from his Essence. Influences coming from the mechanism create personality responses in those whom he reaches. Thus, instead of evoking their spiritual being, the artist stimulates their personality and often leads them in the wrong direction.

Guidance comes from spiritual levels. Thus true creativity is the externalization of the spiritual man.

Many artworks are dead objects; they do not have the life-electricity within them.

A great amount of music carries only the force of the centers below the diaphragm, stimulating the lower centers of the listeners. Such music has a retrogressive effect upon humanity, because the lower centers are already overactive at the expense of the higher centers, and they do not need overstimulation. Many diseases are the result of such overstimulation.

Real creative labor awakens the higher centers and creates balance in the energy network of the human being, which slowly helps man to focus in higher centers to proceed on the path of his evolution.

Sometimes the new level charges your lower centers. If you do not create on the new level but slide down to your normal level through some imagination or thoughtform of low order, the energy in your aura strengthens your imagination or thoughtform of similar low order. In this way you waste your own creative energy in selfish aggressive activities, or in various acts of lower pleasure.

Shakespeare once wrote, "There is a tide in the affairs of men, which, taken at flood, leads on to fortune." If we lose the tide it will be harder for us to catch it. That is why creative people advise us to be ready to hold the tide whenever it comes.

The real tide is the level you reach. From that level, you project your achivement through creative efforts. The gift waves are hitting the shores of our spiritual ocean, but one must be able to raise himself higher and higher to receive them in their crystal purity and beauty.

People must not think that higher levels can be achieved only through meditation and contemplation. One can also contact higher levels through sacrificial service, through enjoying great arts, and through great acts of love and dedication. In these moments one can catch the tide, or a gift wave. If he stays on the wave, if he fuses with it for a period of time, he will experience ecstasy, joy, and a taste of the creative fire.

III. The third labor is to create those movements which will awaken people to raise their level and be creative. For example, one can create a new philosophy, a new religion, a new political activity, a movement for higher freedoms, or a new order which will give man the opportunity to contact the creative energies in his nature.

People create on the mental plane when they think or react mentally. They create on the emotional plane when they aspire, imagine, desire or react with certain emotions. They create physically when they build, when they dance, and when they produce offspring. All living nature creates.

The third labor has three stages:

In the first stage people create under the influence of the forces of nature in a mechanical way. They do not follow their own plan and choice. The varied levels of their achievement have different reactions to these forces, and each reaction or response produces an expression. Creativity is the ability to express, or to produce.

The second stage of creativity is based on personal interests, and does not go beyond the lower mental plane. You have a plan, but it is mostly related to your personal life, to your dreams, loves and different emotions, or to your income, ideology or religion.

The third stage of creativity is based on the hierarchical Plan, and on the Divine Plan. It is a conscious act of creativity to further the Plan on earth through one or more fields of human endeavor. This creativity is carried on in harmony with the highest good for humanity and with the cooperation of the Forces of Light.

This third stage is real creativity. All great talent and genius belongs to this category. They are under the impression of the Plan, and through all that they do they try to bring the Plan into manifestation. Some people in this stage are in contact with creative centers, such as Ashrams on subjective planes, or they are in contact with great Initiates. Others in this stage work directly under the inspiration of their Soul. No matter how they work, you feel a change in your nature when you come in contact with their creative work.

It must be remembered that creativity is not limited to the arts, but it expands through all fields of human endeavor.

Many creative people hide on their level of achievement and are afraid of losing it. Because of the gradually increasing pressure of the common people they either become one of them, or create a new movement which is not above the acceptance level of the masses. Thus they fail to meet their destiny.

The Renaissance was created by those people who achieved a new level. The American revolution was the result of a new awareness.

Creative people must put forces in action to help humanity. The spiritual path is not only the accumulation of knowledge, it is a steady contact with the Infinite Source of creative ideas, a continuous transmutation of these creative ideas, and a labor to put these ideas into action to create greater upliftment, tranformation, and ever-progressive movements.

Thus, when one makes a great amount of money, he does not hide it but puts it into action. Only through using your treasure do you raise your level and accumulate many seeds of experience which you may later change into wisdom.

Let us not forget that your effectiveness is equal to your being-ness. "By the fruits you will know them," said the Great Lord.

Creativeness is the ability to express your highest level of realization or achievement.

A great sage wrote,

"Family, clan, country, union of nations—each unit strives toward peace, toward betterment of life. Each unit of cooperation and communal life needs perfecting. No one can fix the limits of evolution. By this line of reasoning a worker becomes a creator. Let us not be frightend by the problems of creativeness. Let us find for science unencumbered paths. Thus, thought about perfectionment will be a sign of joy."[1]

Creativity requires five elements:

1. knowledge—study
2. energy
3. talent
4. practicality
5. persistence.

1. *Knowledge* is gained through study, observation, and experience. You must enrich your knowledge about the field in which you are working. Partial knowledge is dangerous and it leads to failure. Enriched knowledge leads to greater creativity.

2. *Energy* is a very important factor in our creative life. We are told that in the higher paths of creativity we must economize every drop of our energy in order to be able to use it for the most essential creative service. You must have physical, emotional, and mental energy through economy, rest, and wise usage of it.

3. *Talent* is the result of contact with the Soul. You do not have talent if you are not in contact with the Soul. Your talent increases as you reach greater fusion with your Soul and try to express that fusion creatively.

4. *Practicality* is the ability to relate the Plan to the need. It is the ability to relate the vision to our normal level and raise that level into a higher frequency. Practicality is the sign that "the bridge" in consciousness is constructed, and it now relates the ideas and the translations of ideas to meet the daily needs.

5. *Persistence* is the ability to focus and direct your willpower on your labor until you have finished it. Nothing can be accomplished without steady effort and striving. The greatest labor is the resurrection of the Spirit, and in that great labor you must focus your willpower, forever, to achieve your goal.

Creativity is the ability to give birth to your Divine Self.

Many people fall into depression especially when they are far away from their families or beloved ones, from their hometown or country. This depression becomes deeper at special times such as Christmas, birthdays, and anniversary occasions. It is the result of being lonely or feeling lonely, which is enlarged by pessimistic imagination so that eventually it turns into apathy.

The first step in coming out of such moods or blues is to immediately observe the accumulating clouds of depression.

The second step is to engage oneself in some creative work. For example, play the violin, piano or other instrument, or try to compose some music. If you are not a musician perhaps you can paint, draw, or carve. Or you may sit down and try to write a poem or a letter to the editor of your paper. Or start thinking about a social, political, economical or religious problem, and try to find some solution in your mind.

Or you may play a record and dance, a free original dance, and try to create some new movement to fit the music. Or you may run or swim; or you may sew a dress; build a toy or create something with your hands; or entertain some children; or repair something which needs to be fixed. Another way to help yourself is to jump rope, or go outside and do some deep breathing for ten minutes.

In any case, do not let the clouds accumulate upon you. If you stand alert, you can knock down depression immediately when it starts. If you let it descend upon you, it will be more difficult to get rid of.

When you miss something, you leak and lose energy. Your astral energy flows toward the article you miss. Once you lose a considerable amount of astral and mental energy, loneliness and depression descend upon you.

Creativity shifts the direction of the flow of your energies and uses them in creative activity. As one becomes more creative he generates more energy, and thus raises the level of his joy.

You do not need to be a professional artist to be creative. You just make an effort to be creative. There is the possibility of great creativity if you can hold the emotional tension and sublimate it through your efforts of creativity, labor, or sports.

Many creative people have produced their masterpieces by holding their emotional tension and thus using it.

The Heart

" . . . Creativeness encompasses the fiery potentiality, and is impregnated with the sacred fire of the heart. Therefore, upon the path to the Hierarchy, upon the path of Great Service, upon the path of Communion, synthesis is the one luminous path of the heart. . . . It is precisely the quality of the magnet that is inherent in the heart. The highest creativeness is imbued with this great law. Hence, each consummation, each union, each great cosmic unification is achieved through the flame of the heart . . .

"Thus, we shall keep in memory the beauteous attraction of the magnet of the heart, which links all manifestations."[2]

Chapter 3

CULTURE IN THE NEW AGE

I

REATION IS AN ACT of manifesting beauty. Every part of nature has the same spiritual and innate urge to manifest beauty. In all kingdoms beauty is seen in many forms—in colors, in sound, in movement, in feeling, in thought, in ideas, and in creative expressions.

Human beings are naturally attracted to beauty; they aspire to be beautiful. They want beautiful objects, beautiful expressions, beautiful men, beautiful women, beautiful homes, a beautiful environment. They strive towards beauty. Any achievement on the evolutionary path is an achievement on the path of beauty. Human beings cannot enjoy life without expressing beauty and without living in beauty. Beauty is clearly a food for their souls; it is the most noble urge. A person advances on the path of perfection only through manifesting beauty. Beauty is not only a tonic for those who manifest it, but also a nourishment for those who enjoy it. Beauty heals; beauty expands one's consciousness; beauty transforms one's nature.

Nature creates beauty in great variety—seeds, insects, birds, fish, animals, human beings, stars and galaxies and beyond, all are manifestations of beauty. Beauty is the manifestation of Purpose which underlies all activity in cosmos.

How beautiful are the flowers, the colors and songs of the birds, the colors and movement of fish, the smile of a child, the love of a mother, the courage of a father, the wisdom of a Sage. All this beauty is the manifestation of Divinity in every living form. The Great Life, which we may call God, is the fountainhead of beauty. Beauty in every form is the witness of that Almighty Presence, the presence of that Almighty Life in form. The shortest path to contact God is to contact beauty.

Culture is the translation and interpretation of beauty. It is the objectification and condensation of subjective beauty. The labor to share beauty is culture. When you have culture you have a bridge extending from the Source of beauty to you. It is this that will transform your life as you strive, labor, and eventually penetrate into the mysteries of beauty.

The door to that beauty is within yourself. Your true Self is the door into the ocean of beauty. Any person who becomes self-actualized, anyone that eventually becomes himself—free from all mechanical influences—radiates beauty. As in the universe, in each human being there is hidden the creative beauty, and self-realization is the process of becoming oneself which is a process of creativity and manifestation of beauty. Your Innermost Essence, your Innermost Self, is the Spark of that universal core of Creative Fire. When you are trying to bring that Creative Fire existing within you into manifestation, you are creating culture.

The purpose of culture is Self-generation, birth of the Self, the act of giving birth to the core of your true being.

When the ancients were worshipping fire, they were worshipping the symbol of the Innermost Creative Source in man and in the universe. Culture is the worship of fire. The worship of fire is the process of transformation into fire, and the manifestation of culture results from the effort to transform oneself into fire.

Contact with this fire creates culture. Fire is the symbol of the Source of culture, the symbol of ultimate beauty.

Culture is expressed on four main levels:

1. Personality culture
2. Transpersonal or Soul culture
3. Living or spiritual culture—the culture of the future
4. Culture of the Central Electrical Fire within man and the universe.

The first level of culture is related to the assistance or glorification of the personality—i.e., the physical, emotional, and mental nature of a person. This is expressed in paintings, in sculptures, in poems, in dances and music, and in many kinds of advertisements.

The second level comes into being when the transpersonal Self in man makes its appearance. You can see such appearance in gigantic cathedrals, the writings of Tolstoy, Tagore, Dante and Emerson, the paintings of Michelangelo, the music of Beethoven and Tchaikovsky and other great composers.

The third level of culture is the expression of the Spiritual or rather Divine Fire. Only rare people manifest this beauty. You can see the expression of this culture in the paintings of Nicholas Roerich. This is not personality or soul culture, it is a culture which when contacted immediately releases in some degree the Hidden Divinity within one. A very highly charged energy center is contacted and this energy immediately starts to transform one's nature. This is the fiery culture, the culture of the New Age.

The final culture is the Central Fire in man and in the universe. This culture manifests Itself through the Divine embodiments called Avatars who condense, focus, and radiate the Supreme Transcendental Beauty. An Avatar is a Being who is bringing into birth the Solar Self, and His Culture is a torch on the path of humanity inspiring and directing us towards future evolutions. Such an Avatar is Christ, is Buddha, is Hermes, and other Great Ones.

Personality culture manifests the fire in the physical, emotional, and mental bodies.

Talent manifests the beauty of the Soul.

A genius manifests the fiery beauty of the Spiritual Triad—the beauty of abstract thinking, intuition, and will.

But the Avatar manifests the Innermost Self which is one with the Central Spiritual Sun.

It is very interesting to note that the influence of personality culture is very transient. Yet it does bring some happiness. The culture of talent endures for only minor cycles and brings joy. The culture of the genius lasts long cycles and brings freedom. But the culture of Avatars renews itself age after age. It can keep renewing itself because of the power of the Avatars to raise the level of consciousness of humanity and to increase the ability to interpret culture.

The culture of Avatars brings bliss and striving for humanity; brings revelations for humanity towards which walk all those who are awakening into the reality of such a culture.

Personality culture is the result of the fire of friction, of excitement or contact with personality vehicles or with their centers or spheres which are selfishly manipulated and used for separative purposes. The best example of such a culture is the contemporary advertisement system which is a propaganda system which sells the body and relates to one's emotions. Even academic mental studies through literature, poetry, dance, and music glorify one's own country or nation, or advertise its religion, philosophy, and so on. Much of humanity is in this culture.

Some of the human family have passed into Soul culture, which is the expression of a higher fire that is sometimes called Soul-fire, or the fire of the mental plane and Soul.

The third culture is the result of the fire of the Spiritual Triad.

The fourth one is the result of the Central Electrical Fire. A few in humanity are entering into this division of creativity; this is the division that may be called the culture of the New Age. More and more creative people will enter into this domain and reveal the Innermost Beauty hidden within man.

This revelation and expression of electrical fire or fire of the Innermost Beauty is not only the privilege of artists. The result of such a contact can be expressed through any field of human endeavor. It is not the form of expression that is of major importance, but the voltage of purity, or the energy of goal-fittingness which tunes in with the Plan and Purpose. For example, it can express itself in politics or in the sciences; through new methods of guidance and leadership; new laws; or through new inventions which raise the level of human beings.

Culture is the revelation, the expression and the manifestation of the Hidden Beauty latent within ourselves. This beauty was initially an outpouring expressed through personality culture, and such a culture was indeed necessary because it acts to integrate the personality.

Thus we have four main stages in the expression of beauty. The first is the stage of the neophyte who is eager to produce beauty, but mainly he is used by influences to produce those forms of art which serve separative or selfish purposes. This is the man or woman who is still living within the boundary of his personality vehicles. Such art is transient, although the effect can continue for a long time.

The second stage is the manifestation of beauty by a talent. The talent is a person who is able to penetrate closer to the sanctuary within himself and bring out, to a certain degree, the Sacred Fire of the transpersonal Self, of the Soul.

Then we have a higher degree of creativity, or the manifestation of beauty through a genius. A genius is a man who is able to contact the fire of the Spiritual Triad and bring out through all his expressions the symphony of light, love, and power. Any contact with the work of a genius evokes a great response from your inner resources and you pass through a period of adjustment and transformation.

The fourth stage is the manifestation of beauty by an Avatar. An Avatar is a fully bloomed Spark who is in conscious contact with the Great Principles and Laws of the Solar System. He bridges all that he contacts with that Great Source of glory and creativity. He brings Purpose into life with all that He does. Such Avatars appear cyclically. Their appearances create great cultures and civilizations which last many thousands of years. They are "the Word made flesh."

Avatars bring with them such a great voltage of beauty into the life of humanity, that humanity as a whole moves onto a higher level of its evolutionary path. Any direct or indirect contact with an Avatar causes you to contact the Beauty Within yourself.

A cultured person is one who is in contact with such creative individuals. A cultured person is one who at least is able to appreciate the creativity of a talent and who strives to express that creativity through all his relationships.

In all ages the personality culture assisted in integrating the personality of the man, which revealed to a certain degree, the inner beauty throughout the lower nature.

In this age, as a result of such a culture, many millions of people have integrated their personalities, or are in the process of integrating them so as to be able to go forward for the utilization or the appreciation of Soul-culture.

Personality can be defined as the sum total of our physical, emotional, and mental natures; aligned and integrated in such a way that it acts as a unit in itself. When a person becomes a personality, he must have a large measure of control over his physical urges and drives; sex, food, smoking, sleep, labor, and others. He must have a high degree of control over his emotional nature; and have definite control over his thoughts and speech.

When these three natures of a person are coordinated, they are now ready to give birth to the next level of culture which is Soul-culture. Soul-culture cannot manifest Itself or be appreciated and assimilated when we do not have the foundation of an integrated personality.

Soul-culture brings into fusion the personality with the transpersonal Self, with the Soul and with Its vision of inner beauty, and Its spiritual aspirations.

This culture can be seen, for example, in the Notre Dame Cathedral in Paris; in the magnificent cathedrals in Milan and in Germany; and in the writings of great documents of high statesmanship; or in the paintings of great artists.

Such a culture uplifts human beings and creates Soul-infused personalities. For example, when you are enjoying a great work of music or a great painting you can feel that your level of beingness is slowly rising and your consciousness is entering into another dimension. Your personality is filled with a new thrill, with a new life and joy. That is the result of Soul-infusion through art and culture. This is how you advance from the level of personality vehicles and enter into the Soul domain, and thus surpass your former level of beingness.

The next stage of culture will take you from your Soul level and enable you to contact the Greater Fire of Divinity latent within yourself. This will be the new age culture, the expression of a greater degree of Divinity within you. When this fire expresses itself there is created a very advanced culture which evokes the Divine nature of those who contact it.

As we stated before, cultured people are those people who have a contact with their Inner Divinity to a certain degree. Culture is not education. Education is knowledge, data, information, and the understanding of how to use this information.

Culture is transformation, self-actualization. One can be educated, yet not be cultured. Education is the collection of facts; culture is transformation of one's nature. Culture cannot be created through knowledge only, but through the transformation of life. Education is our society's way of gaining material things; education is the study of culture. The whole subject of education is civilization and culture. Culture is the manifestation of beauty. Beauty is the result of contact with the Innermost Self. Education can learn about culture but it cannot create it unless man transforms himself.

Education is happiness.

Beauty is beingness.

Culture is manifestation of that stage of beingness.

Beauty is bliss.

Culture is joy.

Culture is the expression of beauty, in any form, in any degree.

People have to express beauty to survive. To express beauty means to live progressively on higher levels of being.

To express beauty means to nourish oneself physically, emotionally, mentally, and spiritually by the Inner Fire. As man expresses beauty he recharges himself, charging himself with energy. This energy makes him able to strive to higher levels of beingness and awareness.

The Inner Spark must go forward, and for this act it needs energy, which is produced only when a person creates friction with the Inner Beauty, so as to express it. As he expresses beauty the vehicles of man are charged with energy.

In beauty there is symmetry in measures, in colors, in sound, in movement, in harmony with the related objects or elements.

Beauty evokes responses from the Inner man, from the Self of the planet, and from the Self of the solar system.

It is the Self of man, the planet, and solar system that conceives the prototypes of beauty, and whenever and whatsoever ways and forms a beauty is expressed, that beauty brings responses from those Selves in the form of energy, blessings, and inspiration.

For example, let's assume that in the mind of the Solar Lord there is the thoughtform, or the prototype, of a flower or a symphony. This prototype is projected into space and passes through many spheres, eventually finding an expression on the physical level through the agency of nature—or man. When this prototype is manifested in a high degree of accuracy, it evokes a great current of energy from the actual prototype which radiates through the beauty to those who can contact the beauty—or form.

All expression is as a dance to *music*. If it is synchronized with music in symmetrical formations, there is beauty. The life of beauty is motive and purpose. Each beauty is itself a striving towards a greater beauty. This places the beauty in an extreme discipline—to fuse—to sacrifice itself—to form a part of a greater beauty. In this process diversity is harmonized by the rhythm of purpose.

Cosmic principles control the Laws of color, sound, movement, and measures. Any violation of these Laws creates discord in manifestation. Even man in his Essence is a *sound*, subject to the Laws of Sound. A life lived in harmony with these Laws is beautiful, which means that life is healthy, joyful, creative, symmetrical, synchronized—conscious.

Thus at the center of a human being there exists the Original Beauty, the Self, immaculate and pure.

When this Beauty radiates, the vehicles feel bliss, because It is Life.

This experience of bliss is shared through creating culture, which is a worship of the Innermost Source of Creative Fire, the Self.

Culture is the source of joy. Culture is the joy of life. Freedom is the expression of joy.

Great Conductors of the Symphony of the universe are the Cosmic Principles of the Laws of measure, color, sound, and movement. Man is to learn *himself* to be the conscious and synchronized part of that Cosmic Symphony. Man must play his part, physically, emotionally, mentally, and spiritually to fit into that orchestra and be a part of the Grand Symphony. Each man is a musical instrument. His destiny is to tune his instrument with all the other musicians, in such a progressive way that eventually he will be able to play the seven major and 42 minor notes of the Symphony. His effort will be to express his Divine Self which is one with the Self of the cosmos.

When Great Entities come into manifestation they bring with them a tremendous voltage of beauty and culture and through such beauty and culture they transform the life of the planet. The culture that such great Avatars bring is the culture of the future; the culture of unity; synthesis—one humanity in harmony with the Plan and Purpose behind the Solar System. This is the New Age Culture.

A person must express or manifest beauty to keep himself alive and vital. The greatest vitamin is created through manifesting your Inner Beauty into culture. The greatest power or energy that man can tap is the Fire Within. Once this fire begins to flow into our personality vehicles they are energized correctly and in right proportion, provided that the personality is Soul-infused.

Many people put their hopes in vitamins, but even vitamins cannot be digested if the psychic energy or energy of the Inner Fire is not present in the personality vehicles. And this energy is the one that, flowing out from the Inner Fire, creates culture.

Every time we contact true culture we are energized and revitalized. This is how a sunset or sunrise affects us. That is what a great book or a great painting or music does for us.

We know that in an atom there is a tremendous condensation of energy. But in the human being there is a condensation of cosmic energy. The most important thing for us to do is to release this energy, intelligently and with wisdom. Then we will have the greatest source of nourishment—the nourishment of beauty and its manifestation, culture.

The Divine Fire or Spark within us is the Source of all culture in all its forms, and culture is the manifestation of Divinity or the birth of Divinity. Hence creative people were recognized as Divinely inspired people.

When this Divine Spark begins to release Itself, the little cells in your body and the atoms of all your emotional and mental bodies are charged and nourished. This is a self-charging phenomena. In the very near future a person will realize that he does not need to eat because to eat means to infringe upon life forms.

If you are eating meat you are killing animals, if you are cutting vegetables or flowers this is another kind of violation of life. Whatever you eat you are devouring its Essence to nourish your vehicles. A Master or Avatar does not need to eat. And when we achieve a certain degree of development we will not eat, for the energy within us, through a kind of atomic release process, will sustain our vehicles as nuclear reactors do in atomic energy plants.

As we have the age of atomic power release, we also have the subjective age of the release of the Inner Fire, the Inner Divinity, the Inner Beauty.

What is beauty? Beauty is the Inner Spark through which the whole cosmos is reflected. Cosmos means the harmonization of energy and matter through a progressive Purpose.

Beauty is progressive development and perfection.

Beauty is striving towards perfection.

Beauty is labor to touch higher levels of perfection.

Beauty is direct contact with love, light, and power. When this contact is manifested we call it culture.

Culture is the footprints of the soul which walk toward beauty, toward the Self.

Beauty is called culture because it is the result of the worship of fire, the highest principle in man and the universe.

Beauty is harmony—which is synthesis and diversity in unity.

The enjoyment of culture sublimates and transforms one. It is possible to become clearer in thinking, more loving in relationships, and more energetic in all expressions. Through all these expressions one radiates joy.

The prime quality of a culture is upliftment and transfiguration. The true culture leads toward cooperation, unity and synthesis; toward happiness, joy, and bliss.

Culture integrates and brings one together. Culture opens one to greater insights, deeper visions, and a greater willingness to serve and sacrifice for humanity.

Culture makes one highly creative. The true higher culture causes expansion, and brings one into harmony with all universal manifestation. The races that are the most cultural assist the planet in reaching its destination, to fulfill its purpose as one unified whole. Animal-man progressed and became human through culture; and then man advanced on his path through the process of initiation.

Initiation is nothing else than putting a man in contact with his Inner Beauty. If a person begins to contact that Inner Beauty by 10 percent, he is an aspirant. If that contact is 50 percent, he is a disciple. If it is 75 percent, he becomes an initiate. If it is 100 percent, he is a Master; he becomes Himself. Your true Self is the Master, and that Master can manifest through mastering all that is not his true Self.

Higher culture cannot be assimilated by people who are not refined in their consciousness. Our consciousness is refined when we continuously come in contact with outer and Inner Beauty and try to manifest it in our relationships. That is why culture must be presented in degrees.

First, we must present personality culture for the masses. Then, Soul-culture must next be presented. Finally we must present the fiery culture of the new age, which is fusion with our Essential Fire.

There is no cultural manifestation without heavy labor. To bring your real Self out into expression is not an easy job. It takes courage, daring, striving, and heavy labor.

The time of contact with the beauty within you is a time of highest transformation, fusion, and creativity—a time in which one enters into the sphere of his own Divinity. He becomes for a while a creator, a superman. If these short moments of contact increase and become the whole life then man is the culture itself, the Avatar, and in all His expressions the cosmos finds manifestation. Cosmos means harmony between energy and matter, and spirit and form, through an advancing purpose.

As in the individual, so are the Great Lives laboring to manifest beauty, greater beauty. Thus, the creation of a solar system is a way for a Great Life to bring out that which is within Him; through a solar system, His achievement and His cosmic contact are manifested and realized. And we know that solar systems are always in process of formation as the vehicles of expressions of Great Lives. The Great Lives are always in labor to create greater systems and galaxies, in which our solar system is but a speck, or an atom.

Every living form in the nature is engaged in this great process of manifesting beauty, from the tiny atom to the Great Lives which are called galaxies.

Beauty manifests as culture, and culture manifests as civilization. Culture is the partial expression of beauty in time and space, and civilization is the utilization of culture in our daily life. For example, all our music and painting and philosophy is part of our culture. All of our TV stations, atomic reactors, electrical instruments, hospitals, communication systems, are part of our civilization.

Intuitives contact beauty; creative people translate it into culture. Practical idealists build it into a civilization.

We contact beauty according to what we are. Our understanding and degree of expressing beauty is our own measure. And because our measure of perfection is far away from being equal to the Solar and Cosmic Lives, it necessarily follows that all our culture is relative. As a person progresses on the path of perfection, he will give birth to higher and higher cultures.

It is interesting to note that beauty is one, but the manifestations of beauty are many. We have many cultures on many levels, but they are all efforts to manifest the same beauty. It is similar to a person who tries very hard year after year to manifest or externalize his own Self, which is one, but in manifestation this oneness takes many different forms.

In all forms of culture you touch the same beauty. And when you contact beauty you contact your real Self. The true beauty is manifestation of Self. And the true culture is the culture that leads you to your real Self through transforming and transfiguring your vehicles of manifestation. Transformation of your nature is the first sign that you are assimilating culture.

Why is it that the true culture causes transformation? It is because culture carries the voltage, the charge, the frequency of your higher being. Your higher being is seldom in the state of radioactivity due to the many forms of pollution within your aura. But when you contact culture, the higher frequency lights the inner fires and your inner being begins to radiate out, cleansing and transforming your being.

To live means to give manifestation to the innermost fire of life within you. When this fire manifests, you exist, you live. You live not as your vehicles but as your Self. The innermost Self within you must come into expression and that is what the abundant life is. Immediately when your innermost Self stops manifesting you are in the process of dying. Immediately when a person stops expressing his Inner Divinity, beauty, joy, goodness, truth, and simplicity, he is dead. He becomes a floating corpse.

Culture is based on labor and striving. Striving is a continuous effort to contact your true Self to touch progressively the deeper and deeper layers of that Inner Divinity. Our labor is a continuous effort to bring that contacted level of Divinity into manifestation.

When we cease to be identified with our vehicles, then our true Self radiates out. This is the secret of all artists. When they are not identified with their physical, emotional, and mental vehicles and with their associated inertias, glamors, illusions, irritations, and fears then they manifest great beauty through their arts and bring in a high voltage culture to the world.

Sacred dances are a great means to disidentify ourselves from the triple worlds. Try to manifest the meaning, the purpose of the music and of the dance, which for that moment may give one the experience of being something different than the personality.

We appreciate culture according to our level. Slowly we feel the transforming power of the culture. If you are watching a great dancer and your consciousness is not very elevated you might say, "What beautiful legs she has." If you are a little higher you might say, "The harmony between music and movement is very thrilling." If you are more exposed to the Inner Light you might say, "My goodness, this dance reveals so many secrets in me, and I see now how the parts of the jigsaw puzzle are coming together and solving so many psychological problems in me." And if you are yet higher, you will feel complete bliss and enlightenment. You will see the clear path you should take; you will see the nonsense of your problems, fears, and anxieties and will enter into a stage of fearlessness, radioactivity, and service. These are the moments of great inspiration in which your true Self reveals Itself.

The true culture will eliminate from the world the entire trash in which we are living—the crimes, the deceptions, exploitations, hypocrisy, greed, fear, selfishness, and their like.

It is very important also that people expose themselves to culture gradually. We have seen persons who run away from beauty or from creative people; the voltage is too much for them. They can develop an antagonism if we force them to contact cultural phenomena. If the capacity of a person's reception is limited then he becomes overflooded and feels irritated because he cannot assimilate the beauty and his nature either hates, or uses the mechanism of rejection. There is also the psychological fact that when faced with a great beauty some people develop an intense fear. This is very interesting because in great beauty a person loses himself. The small self to which he was attached must go however, if he really wants to enjoy the beauty. This sensation of course translates itself as fear if a person is to some degree identifying with his physical, emotional, and lower mental world.

Exposure to great beauty is like throwing oneself into the ocean; first there is fear, but then once you lose that fear you experience joy and identification with the ocean.

Jealousy has the same foundation. One day in a monastery where I was living, a highly evolved man came to speak to us. He was very handsome and impressive. When I saw him on the stage with his beautiful robe, I said to myself, "He is nothing; what is great in him?" Then I observed myself and said, "What are you talking about? He is so beautiful." Then the dialogue continued within myself. I said "No, he is not beautiful, he is showing off." Another conversation entered, "You are crazy; you are jealous. Listen, look at him with your Higher Self. No," I said, "he is not beautiful because I am not standing there in his place. He is not me." Again the dialogue changed. "That man is *me*, I love *him*. I am a bud, he is the flowering. I love him."

It was after this inner dialogue that I began to hear the man's inspiring and uplifting words, because *he became me*, and there was no danger of losing myself.

At the time of any cultural enjoyment, if you observe your actions, reactions, and responses you learn much about your psychology and expose yourself to a greater light. To unite progressively with beauty, through culture, means to lose your not-self and become your true Self.

Christ once said that those who want to find themselves must lose themselves. This is a profound, deep wisdom that Christ gave us. The little self must be lost, so that the greater Self reveals Itself. This is easily understood when we remember that in our childhood we have our teddy bears, with which we were totally identified. But as we grow in our consciousness we choose new teddy bears appropriate to our level. Our cars, books, school, wives, husbands, girlfriends, boyfriends, are new teddy bears; even our business and art are teddy bears. But if you want to proceed toward perfection, your teddy bears, gradually and respectfully, must be replaced by higher ones. This is what culture does.

Our first selfishness is a teddy bear, and we cannot live without it. Then we replace it with family selfishness. Later we replace this by racism, nationalism. Until one day we think in terms of one humanity, one solar system, one galaxy. This is what the true culture does. It causes one to renounce onself from ones limitation and face Infinity.

Sometimes we cannot contact beauty because we feel ashamed in front of a great expression of beauty. Also we cannot contact beauty if we feel excessive excitement. Both of these feelings interfere with our coming into contact with beauty. The reason for this is that when you feel shame, you are identified with your shortcomings or failures, or with acts and actors within you that produced that shame. If you are excited you are not allowing the energy of beauty to be absorbed into your higher system, because excitement is identification with the result of the higher contact, but not with the Self itself. In all these conditions one enters the field of beauty with fear and rejection because in each of these situations you are losing a part of your lower self. But in the meantime you are finding your true Self which sometimes creates violent reactions from the lower self.

Separativeness greatly diminishes the life current and the joy of life. Expansion towards unity, towards Infinity is the process of self realization, which is an act of finding your true Self, in greater unity and synthesis. We have the simplest example of this fact in our body. If any part of the body separates itself from the interests of the rest, the body sickens or starts dying. If all parts work for each other, all parts are happy in unity, and you are healthy and alive. The beauty and strength of the body is in its unity. That is what culture teaches us on a global scale. It provides the ways and means for unification and synthesis. Wholeness is health, happiness, and joy. Wholeness means that the parts are serving the whole, and the whole is serving the parts. This fact, if understood internationally would solve all our political and social problems.

To produce great cultures a nation or a group of highly creative people must have no discord within the system. Only a unified field of energy can create and manifest beauty. This is why the great creative people also are called saints. These people are harmonized or are in tune with the Divinity within themselves, or with the Divinity in nature.

The creative process and the enjoyment of culture demands refinement, purification, and a tuning in with the Divine Presence in nature and man. Creativity is the result of unification, at-onement, and fusion.

Let us repeat, personality culture is the result of the integration of our personality vehicles. Soul culture starts when personality fuses itself with the transpersonal Self. The next stage is at-onement with the Innermost Fires within you, by which you can manifest the true culture in harmony with the Divine Purpose and intent.

The intention of all creative people in the world must be to establish a world-cultural month, during which all nations will share the culture of all other nations. This also must be planned in such a way that the nations who for certain reasons had war or are antagonistic towards each other, must especially demonstrate the culture of the nations they hate. A steady cultural exchange will then be established between nations which slowly pave the way for peace, for one world, and for one humanity.

In Agni Yoga we read: ". . . Our Command is to miss no opportunity of reminding people about culture."[1]

Let us discuss what the effect of culture is and let us see what a cultured person does:

1. A cultured person charges other human beings with an uplifting, regenerating energy which cheers them up, energizes and makes them enjoy life. This energy charge is a combination of light, love, intuition, and will. It is light, a sunshine pouring upon human beings.

2. The cultured person is a healing agent through which the healing energies of nature radiate out—integrating, aligning, and fusing the physical, emotional, and mental nature of other people in proportion to the intensity and the level of the energy. Such an alignment and fusion allows psychic energy to circulate throughout the human system, healing and purifying the whole system. Many people are healed when they have a real contact with beauty. Beauty

releases the Fiery Essence of man, which is the only true agent of healing.

3. The cultured person creates right-human-relations. He is for harmony, for unity, for understanding. I remember a lady whose husband was in prison and she never visited him because she hated what he did. One day, we took her to the Music Center to enjoy the performance of the Swan Lake ballet. It was a tremendous performance. When we were leaving the Center she held my hands, looked into my eyes and said, "I would like to visit my husband, if you would be kind enough to take me there." "Of course," I replied.

Culture breaks separative walls between people, walls made by prejudices, emotions, thoughts, and traditions. CULTURE BRIDGES THE HEARTS.

Most of our ill health is caused by the separative thoughts in our minds, thoughts which prevent right-relations between the organs of our bodies, and between man and man, between nation and nation.

Separative thoughtforms are like clouds hanging between the earth and the sun. When we disperse this obstruction we have the rays of the sun, vitality, and right-human-relationships because the energy of life is released and life energy always seeks to unify. Thus a cultured person is a Fiery Essence, burning out all separative walls between nations and races.

Creativity is conditioned by the state of unity in consciousness and the energy field in which man lives. Once you are separative within yourself, you lose the power to create. Ever-flowing creativity in nature is the proof of a source of unity behind nature. The more you are unified the more you create, in increasing higher quality.

When the electricity of culture flows through man releasing the power of beauty within, it creates unity and wipes away all separative walls that exist within one's nature. When the separative walls are eliminated from the physical, emotional, and mental mechanisms there will be no reason for sickness for essentially we are Divine, essentially we are part of God, essentially we are Him. Then why are there all these manifold separations between man and man, nation and nation? Because we are identified with our separate vehicles and with their interests, and we think that we can live only at the expense of others. Culture heals this sickness, because it releases the beauty from all of us, and in that beauty we see our unity and our Divinity. The day will come in which we will realize that the language of God is the language of beauty. At that stage we will be able to see Him in the eyes of a child, in the songs of the birds, in the colors of flowers, in the expression of supreme art. When we manifest this sense of unity, this sense of oneness, we will have right-human-relations and goodwill.

4. Culture creates INTERNATIONAL unity. Beauty urges you to cooperate, to share, even to renounce; beauty breaks the separative walls.

I remember well a young man who often spoke to me about a nation that he said he really hated. One day he visited me in the company of a girl who was a member of the nation that he despised.

"How come," I asked, "you are with her?"

"You know," he said, "she is beautiful no matter what background she has. I love her beauty."

Isn't that beautiful? The great artist Nicholas Roerich once said, "THROUGH BEAUTY WE CONQUER," and the greatest victory is a victory over separative men. To conquer means to be beautiful. Thus culture creates international unity.

5. In the process of creating beauty and culture we eventually contact a Plan, and behind the plan a Purpose. A talented person or a genius is one who intuitionally sees that there is a Plan for humanity, and that there is a Purpose in this creation. When a talented person or genius creates, he is in tune with some Inner Source of blueprints, some Inner directions, which are inspiring him and charging him to go ahead and create culture. A talented person sees a Plan for whole humanity. A genius sees the Purpose behind it. An Avatar unites with the Will behind the Purpose.

Culture is the manifestation of the Plan, of the Purpose, of the Will of the Great Source from Whom everything proceeds, and to Whom everything returns.

6. Through culture we develop sensitivity to great ideas and directions coming from Higher Sources.

7. Through culture we expand our consciousness and become more inclusive. The age of synthesis will be entered through ever-developing culture and beauty.

How can we start enjoying beauty and culture? The first step is

OBSERVATION. Observe beauty wherever you find it. Take a flower in your hand, enjoy the form of the petals, colors, fragrance. Listen to the singing birds; watch the trees, lakes, mountains, waterfalls—the beauty in nature. As you contact beauty in nature the more you become your true Self. Then observe beauty in other human beings, in whatever way it manifests itself. Next, observe and enjoy the culture of as many nations or races as possible. This will expand your horizons and make you more humble and more harmless. Observation of beauty is an effort to identify with the beauty within oneself. That moment when one admires beauty is the moment of transformation.

Once I was visiting a family and talking with the man who had a most beautiful wife. A little later the wife brought tea to us, and when she gave the cup to her husband, he like a frozen fish murmured under his nose, "Thank you." I noticed that "thank you" and said, "My gosh, why did you not first look at her face and give her a big smile, and with a sweet and joyful voice say, 'thank you?'" "So what!" he said.

Appreciation of beauty increases beauty; negation or refusal of beauty pulls one back down to his selfish and separative nature where joy and creativity are absent. Appreciate beauty in each other if you want to increase understanding, joy, and success in your family. When you appreciate beauty you are affirming the Divinity within each other; you are contacting the Divine Presence within each other and trying to bring it into manifestation.

We are not yet really born. Our physical nature is there, but our Divine nature is only in manifestation a small percentage. WE— our true, Innermost Self—is in process of birth. The Innermost Beauty is slowly, slowly coming into manifestation, and as it manifests through all that you are and do, you become the *beauty* in manifestation. The first step is to observe beauty, to admire beauty, to adore beauty, worship beauty. This is how you can unify yourself with the source of beauty sleeping within you.

Once I asked two hundred students if they ever watched a sunset or sunrise. Only fifteen of them said yes. The others were surprised I had even asked such a question. They had never been exposed to such beauty! We must take our children into nature and show them mountains, trees, sunsets, lakes, canyons, flowers, and seeds. The beauty of nature will make them really human, and will enable them to throw off the pollution accumulated in their aura from the effects of most of the movie and television programs and contaminated publications.

The second thing that we must do is to bring into our homes beautiful music, paintings, beautiful furniture, and radiant harmonious colors which will elevate the spirit and nourish it.

Actually beauty is a source of energy, a vitamin. Where there is beauty there is a continuous flow of energy. People who are engaged in fine art or with the expression of beauty are mostly energetic, enthusiastic, and radioactive.

Take your children into great music centers, let them hear symphonic music, enjoy ballets, dramas, and song festivals; have them see great paintings, architecture, and sculpture; have them participate in ceremonies in beautiful cathedrals. All of these will help them have a new birth, because they will release the nucleus of life within them which will energize and strengthen all their nature.

Pregnant women especially should stay in close contact with beauty in all forms. They should listen to great lectures and participate in high level seminars. Their babies will be special, because the elevated thought will affect the embryo and condition his or her future growth in the right direction. The embryo very closely shares the experiences of the mother, and if the mother is exposed to beauty the baby will instinctively search for beauty and find the sources of higher joy.

We must also exercise the manifestation of beauty in all our expressions—while we are talking, walking, dancing or in anything that we do. This is not easy, but the reward is great. Beauty is truth, righteousness, kindness, love, harmlessness, simplicity, accuracy, harmony. Beauty is often renunciation, detachment, Divine indifference, selflessness. Let us try all of these through all of our expressions, and then we will see the transformation of our nature.

If we do not have light, love, truth—but instead have lies, gossip, criticism, curses, crimes—we will not have beauty, but ugliness; because beauty is goodness, love, truth, reality.

Of course, all these things must be penetrated into and recognized through a life of meditation. Meditation is the labor for beauty. Meditation slowly dissipates ugliness, attachment, maya, glamors, and illusions and carries you to the sunshine. Meditation is an act of raising your consciousness out of your personality limitations and pollutions, and fusing it with your Spiritual Essence. Meditation is first the process of contact with the Divine Presence in the universe, and then the act of formulating this contact into culture in such a way or in such a form, that you build a path for other people to reach beauty.

Culture is the result of contact with the Divine Sources of energy within you, and within the universe. Then we have discipline. Actually discipline is nothing else but the coordination of your physical, emotional, and mental life to the laws and principles of your Innermost Being. When the channels of communication clear between your vehicles and the Source of life within you, we say that a person is under discipline. Through such a discipline a person eventually becomes a disciple. And a disciple is a person who commits himself and his life to the perpetual flow of electricity from that Innermost Beauty, from the Source of life and creativity.

Discipline is the act of eliminating all hindrances which prevent the expression of beauty, or the act of coordination and fusion of the bodies with the fountainhead of creativity within, so that greater inspirations and greater fire pour down and transform the world conditions.

There is a poem which says, "Kalagiya, Come to Shamballa".[2]

Kalagiya is Sanskrit, meaning come to the Tower. The Tower is the Divinity within yourself. Enter into your own Tower and be your true Self. Do not wander in the valley of darkness, ugliness, and illusions but come and unite with your Essence, with beauty.

Culture leads toward self exertion because the Divinity within cannot limit itself on our present level. The true nature of Divinity is expansion, and the result of expansion is BEAUTY, is the sense of Infinity. This comes to all who do not tolerate limitation of the expression of beauty.

CULTURE IN THE NEW AGE

II

CULTURE IS THE MANIFESTATION of the fire of the Spirit. When the Spirit flows down upon the fields of consciousness, it creates culture. It creates the bridge for humanity to pass on to a higher level of awareness. Spirit is fire, and it is the fire that creates.

Culture is the result of a contact with the fire within the universe. This contact releases the hidden mysteries, laws, principles and beauty within the fire.

Aspiration is a form of contact with this Inner Fire.

Meditation is a deeper contact through which the fire finds an opportunity of expression.

Contemplation is an ability to see the mysteries lying within the fire.

Illumination is a process of fusion with the fire, in ever expanding inclusiveness.

Inspiration is the steady inflow of the fire through the vehicles of manifestation.

This is how true culture is manifested. Wherever there is culture, there is the link with higher worlds.

"In the whole history of mankind neither food nor industry, nor intellect unenlightened by the spirit, have ever built up true culture. And it is with special care that we should treat everything that yet may raise the level of the spirit."[3]

Culture is the service of beauty. Culture refines the consciousness and makes man more sensitive to the pulse of the cosmic heart. Through culture people come closer to each other. Through culture the boundaries of races, colors, countries, and religions are eliminated. Culture provides the only language through which races can communicate with each other, and people can understand each other.

Culture may manifest through the characteristics of individual

80

races or nations, but in its essence it is universal, because the source of culture is beauty. When beauty blooms through all human endeavors we have culture. And because beauty is the one concealed Divinity within man and universe, every cultured person and every cultured group is naturally non separative, all inclusive, all loving.

Culture is built through light and increasing light, knowledge, understanding, and through a sense of deeper reality. It is very interesting to know that culture is not static, but it is an ever growing, ever expanding, ever organizing manifestation of beauty.

Cultures of the past will be the syllables of the words of the present age. The words of culture of this age will be sentences of culture of the future. This will go on until the chapter of culture of this solar system is written, which will form, in its turn, a few pages in the book of the scheme. That book will explain the hidden beauty in the heart of the flaming sun.

"If you desire the gates to be opened, pronounce
    My Sign
I said Beauty in combat and victory.
I said Beauty, and failure was covered by Beauty.
Mountains blossomed with Beauty.
And you must open the way for the flowers of Beauty.
Let the children approach and bow
    before Him Who brought the Beauty of the
    great Universe."[4]

Culture is the act of opening the way for the flowers of beauty. There is a great healing power in the as yet unrealized flowers of beauty. Contemplation of beauty is the cure for diseases.

"Blessed are you who aspire to Beauty."[5]

"In Beauty will Infinity be manifested. In Beauty the teachings of the Seekers of the spirit are illumined. In Beauty we do not fear to manifest the truth of freedom. In Beauty do we kindle radiance in every drop of water. In Beauty do we transform matter into a rainbow."[6]

The great Teacher speaking about *imperil* says,

"He who is afflicted with imperil must repeat: 'How beautiful is everything!' And he will be right; because the flow of evolution is rational, in other words, beautiful."[7]

In seeing beauty everywhere and in everything a person comes in contact with the healing and regenerating energies of beauty. We can prove this in meditating and contemplating on beauty whenever our consciousness becomes imprisoned by the conditions of the lower worlds.

All that man does to serve sacrificially, to conduct a life in harmony with the highest spiritual laws, his every act of compassion, of truth, of goodwill, every striving towards the Supreme is the result of blooming beauties within his own chalice. When the Spirit blooms and unfolds in and through the chalice, man becomes a fountain of creativity.

Beautiful lives are the manifestation of beauty within the chalice. Agelong accumulation of the chalice gives birth to great geniuses. Manifested and expressed beauty builds the chalice. Our vehicles are built through what we express. If we express beauty through all our acts, feelings, and thoughts our whole mechanism of expression will be like a symphony, through which Inner Beauty will radiate with its creative healing and enlightening powers.

Communication with cosmos creates culture. Culture conditions the survival of human life because it makes us see the beauty in each other's heart, culture makes us identify ourselves with beauty.

Christ once spoke about lilies which were dressed better than King Solomon. The tradition says that the real sign of a spiritually advanced person is his ability to notice beauty, even if it is hidden in a rag of ugliness. Thus, the tradition says that once when the great Teacher was walking with His disciples, they saw a big crowd. With His disciples He came closer to the crowd to see what was going on. "Master," said one of the disciples, "There is a dead dog, they are throwing stones to bury it." Those who were throwing the stones were expressing their reactions with curses, and commenting how ugly and awful the dead dog was.

Christ looked awhile, turned to His disciples and said, "The dog has teeth like shining pearls."

People who are dead in consciousness see only the ugliness. To see the beauty and to affirm it is an act of gratitude to the Source of life.

"During ascent there is the urgent desire to look beyond the snowy peaks that soar before you . . . It is joyous not only to ascend a summit, but to follow the ways of ascent in thought."[8]

". . . We anticipate a miracle, we strive to break the lock, but the ladder of the Arhat is only in the Beautiful."[9]

"Each striving is saturated with the fire of spirit. The creativeness of the spirit takes part in the fiery consciousness of the Cosmos. How can one be isolated from the entire cosmic creativeness when man is the creative fulfiller of the Cosmic Will? One should therefore develop consonance with the Higher Powers in oneself, for without this striving to consonance there is no creativeness."[10]

People eventually will come to the awareness that beauty is a transmitter of energy. The level of beauty is equal to its voltage of energy. In all ages people drew a great amount of energy from works of art. This energy helped them in many ways.

A. It expanded their consciousness.
B. It released the latent centers from inertia.
C. It harmonized their emotional and mental worlds, and cured the physical body from many disorders.
D. It made them strive towards perfection.
E. It created an optimistic or positive attitude towards life.
F. It made them creative.
G. It gave them a sense of unity.
H. It challenged them to serve, to love, and to sacrifice.

The energy of beauty can even change the character of a person and lead him to the path of total transmutation.

It stimulates higher centers, and puts them in action. Higher centers are channels of higher energies, and link consciousness with the higher worlds.

Each form of beauty has a special message for humanity and a great task for nature. If a man learns how to surround himself or others with the forms of beauty, he can be a great agent of spiritualization and creativity.

Beauty is born through pain. How interesting it is to watch the painful labor through which creative people go. Every time a greater energy of beauty wants to manifest, the artist goes through a fiery tension. There are many oppositions in our nature that arrange themselves to prevent the birth of beauty, and this causes pain. There are many around us who fear the birth of beauty, because it reveals the need for labor and striving. This also causes pain in the artist.

The birth of beauty needs greater space in man, and better conditions in the environment. As the artist expands his space, the little lives of his body ache, and the environment rejects him. This also causes pain to a true creator of beauty. But through all this pain and as a result of it, he expands.

Once Nicholas Roerich said, "Wings, Wings! you grow painfully."[11]

All true creators know what he means. But the suffering, pain, and sacrifice for the cause of beauty eventually release those fountains of bliss which charge every act of creativity with radioactive energy.

Beauty is the nourishment of the whole person. It is the strongest vitamin and tonic, but only if we know how to use it.

Ugliness is a poison to the heart. Any expression of ugliness shortens life, obscures the vision, and darkens the consciousness.

Degeneration of a person or nation, starts with the expression of ugliness. Any action or expression which denies the essential Divinity of man, which rejects the spirit of gratitude and the challenge of cooperation, can be classified as a non-survival factor in the history of humanity. Decomposition of the aura begins with the acts of ugliness.

On the other hand, the energy of beauty heals, uplifts, and enlightens.

One must have daily nourishment of beauty. This nourishment must be as regular as breakfast or dinner, until one learns to live, to exist, and to move in beauty.

When a man is in contact with beauty he is in a process of purification.

The energy of beauty:

A. Purifies the vehicles from obstructions.
B. Balances the centers.
C. Unfolds the consciousness.
D. Gives one the power to be indifferent to any urge or drive toward ugliness.

The energy of beauty can be assimilated abundantly through

meditation and sacrificial service. Beauty has seven notes expressing through seven Rays. Each ray has its own form of beauty and its own way to create beauty.

First Ray beauty puts you in contact with the Purpose, and reveals the synthesis.

The second Ray beauty reveals to you a part of the Plan.

Third Ray beauty initiates you into the field of creative forces.

Fourth Ray beauty shows the creative activities of apparently conflicting forces.

Fifth Ray beauty reveals the process of manifestation of Spirit in the Laws of nature.

Sixth Ray beauty reveals the nature of daring and sacrifice.

Seventh Ray beauty reveals the supreme dance of matter and Spirit.

Any branch of art or science can manifest through any of these rays to create beauty of its own kind.

The whole aim of the creative forces is to manifest the concealed Beauty of the Creator, until all manifestation expresses that Inner Beauty.

"Repeat Beauty again and again, even with tears, until you reach your destiny."[12]

CULTURE IN THE NEW AGE

III

". . . Our command is to miss no opportunity of reminding people about culture."[13]

WHEN WE SPEAK about the new age, we think that the new age is conditioned by dates or cycles, but this is not really so. The new age is a state of consciousness, or rather a state of beingness. The new age is the result of touching the Innermost Realities within ourselves. Any time any person touches the most Supreme Fire within himself, he is in the new age. Although one may live in an age where the majority of people are in intellectual and moral darkness, one can still be in the new age within his own consciousness and realizations.

The new age is not 3000 A.D. or 5000 A.D.—it always *is*. It is up to you to realize it through your achievements.

When a person achieves a high level of awareness, when he ascends the summit of his consciousness or of his spiritual awareness, he enters into a new age. And if his progress is continuous towards Infinity he is always in the new age, just like an object which flies so fast that the sun never sets on it. For such a person, not only is everything he perceives *new*, but also all his creative expressions and responses are new.

Our creativity is the reflection of our inner achievements. Every time we expand our awareness and deepen our realization, our creativity reflects our new achievement. As a person approaches his true Self and creates a more unified field of energy within his being, he becomes more creative because he allows the cosmic creative waves to manifest through him endlessly and in greater beauty and simplicity.

Those who penetrate the domain of Infinity are always in the new age, no matter in what age they live. Christ, Buddha, Zoro-

86

aster, Hercules, are such examples. No matter in what past age They lived, They were thousands of years ahead of us, and They are always in the new age. That is why They are called Sons of Light, because darkness never sets on Them. They became Sons of Light because They touched, fused and became one with the Fire Within, with the Fire of Infinity.

Culture has a very interesting origin. It means the service, the worship, or the veneration of the Inner Fire. Ur, in many languages, means fire or light.

Culture is an expression of contact with the Inner Light or Inner Fire. A cultured man is a man who has contact with his Innermost Self, and is able to express that contact through a creative life. It is highly interesting to note that once people touch the Inner Fire in a certain degree, they walk the path of freedom, and the path of releasing others into freedom. No matter how rich or how smart a man is, no matter how high his position or what influence he has on others, he cannot be called a cultured man if he does not have a steady contact with this Inner Fire, which brings in conflagration and progressively destroys all obstacles on the path of his enlightenment, freedom, beauty, and compassion making him a sacrificial server of the human race.

Fire is everything. Everything in existence is a result of the gradual dimming of the fire. An atom is an extinguished fire, a kind of charcoal, by which all forms on the physical plane are built. We also have the emotional fire, the mental fire, and the fire of the intuition. All is fire on a gradient scale, and the Source of fire, is the *Self*.

First there is the fire of the body. All expressions based on the fire of the body are not culture, unless that fire is used as a channel to express spiritual intent.

We also have the expression of the emotional fire. If you open your television and read your daily paper you can see the expression of this fire—in crimes, in movies that inflame your negative emotions, fear, anger, hatred, blood-thirstiness, cheap sex, and so on. All these are sold to the public in the name of culture.

We also have the fire of the lower mind. The expression of that fire is called "culture"—such as our advertising system, which appeals to the blind instincts in man, or tries to manipulate him through hypnotic suggestions and so forth. All these fires speak in the name of "culture."

Most of what is called culture originates from these lower fires. Most of the art which fills the market, occupies the hours on television, radio, the theater, the stage, and magazines originates from hatred, sex, greed, anger, vanity, ambition, depression, self-pity, fear, envy, and so on. On the other hand, we have those art expressions which originate from the Inner Fire, which is the will-to-serve, the will-to-uplift, the will-to-illuminate, the will-to-awaken, the will-to-sacrifice and be one with Light.

Actually, the creative process is a process of unification and at-one-ment with oneself. Once the heart absorbs the Light from the intuitional or higher planes, that person becomes a cultured person, because the fire that is coming from his Innermost Essence will purify his physical, emotional, and mental nature. When a person is purified he is healthy, he is beautiful, harmonious, peaceful, kind and noble, because that Inner Fire not only purifies but also enlightens. Enlightenment is a continuous process of expansion of awareness of the Plan and Purpose of the Great Life.

A really cultured person is a person of enlightenment. After such an achievement that person can give something real to the world. Before such an enlightenment all of his expressions are based on glamors, illusions, and on blind urges and drives within him. We have higher fires within us. They are the intuitional, the atmic, and the monadic fires, which are the real mechanisms through which the Spark of Life, our true Self, manifests.

One uses these fires according to ones degree of achievement. If one is attracted to the lower fires, and is using them for his separative activities, the life he is creating is not a life of culture, is not a life of radioactivity, but a self-oriented, separative and even a self-destructive activity. But if one is fused with the higher fires, all that one does, all that one feels and thinks, will build up the real culture of humanity. For in that culture one will see the worship of Light, the worship of Life, and the vision of the future.

Creativity is the ability to express these higher fires in such a way that people are inspired to expand their consciousness. They are inspired to organize their lives as a service for others. They are inspired to bring into manifestation the Great Beauty sleeping within their hearts, and express great reverence to the Spark of life in every human being.

Culture is a fiery activity to purify the inertia, the glamors, and illusions of the ages, accumulated within the human nature through identification with the lower fires. Once the personality fires are purified by the higher fire, one is on the path of transfiguration, or on the path of enlightenment.

The real culture of humanity is given by those who are able to penetrate into the higher fiery domains, achieve enlightenment or transfiguration, and present to humanity those great values through which humanity not only can survive, but can progress towards its cosmic destination. These higher values are those principles which radiate from a central Plan, from a central Purpose, and relate humanity to its future glory.

Before a man achieves such a degree of enlightenment, all his creative endeavors are based upon his glamors, illusions and vanities, and he really can give nothing to humanity except confusion, doubt, and slavery.

The leadership of a nation is its culture. Culture leads the nation to its future. Only in culture is the vision grasped, because culture is the messenger of the vision, and is the worship and the expression of beauty.

The great Sage M.M. says, "The new era can be built only by means of culture. Therefore, culture will be proclaimed as the one defense against disintegration."[14]

It is only a vision of the future that holds people together. This is so true that it can be applied to any form created in the universe by nature or by human hands.

Those forms of life that do not express the future Plan and Purpose of the Great Creator slowly disintegrate and disappear from the surface of the earth. All those man-made forms that no longer serve His Purpose are abandoned, destroyed and cast away. To be obsolete means to have no future, or be unable to fit in with a future construction or plan.

Culture is the magnetic cement of a form, the future vision in the form, and the path of progress through life towards Infinity.

A true culture is not limited by time, race, or environment. In every true culture there is a note which belongs to all ages; a rhythm that belong to all races; and a color that fits all environments.

All those who create such a culture live in the Infinite Domain. They prove their immortality through their culture, and stand against the disintegrative power of time and change.

We have seen for centuries how the nations by changing their political personnel, by conquering territories, by raiding their financial resources and advancing their industry, did not really progress. All of these can even work against their survival. But nations do progress and enjoy their prosperity if they are built on a solid foundation of culture.

A new era begins when we live a life of higher cooperation, unity, understanding and with a more sensitive response to the creative forces in man and in nature. Many cycles will come and pass, perhaps on higher and higher spirals, but man will never have a true response to the energies and opportunities present in them, unless he consciously expands his consciousness and manifests his contact with these energies of new cycles in his creative life.

When certain forms of life become unable to respond to the energies and opportunities of the new cycle for a period of time, they are cast away, and become extinct. This holds true for animal forms, as well as human beings, races and nations, and even for globes, solar systems and galaxies.

The form is held together only by the magnetic influence of that mysterious thing which we call Purpose. If the Purpose of existence fades away, the form disintegrates. The Purpose in each form is the fire which leads the form towards continuous renewal, adaptation, and creativity.

The "survival of the fittest," is the ability of a *life form* to renew the flow of fire, or life-forces within, through creative discrimination, adaptation, and expression of beauty.

Many members of the human family may live in the Aquarian Age, but they will never be in tune with it. It is even possible that the energies provided by the Aquarian Age will be misused by them and against the real intent of the age, because man translates the energy according to his own level, or according to his response mechanism.

Thus, those who are not new age people will not be in the new age. Only a new age person makes the age a new age and creates a new culture. The new culture is nothing else but his experiences with his Innermost Self. It is through such an exalted state of awareness that he sees the deeper values, deeper relationships, and deeper significances of life.

Everything is. It is now a matter of contacting a part, or the totality of it.

If, five thousand years ago, a person perceived what we are seeing now, he would have been new age at that time and would be considered our contemporary. Those who are two thousand years ahead are in the new age even if they are younger than we are.

When we speak of leadership, we refer to the ability of a person to see as far as two thousand years ahead. Only such a person can be a leader, because he sees present events in the light of the future. A cultured person is a person of leadership, because he makes us see beyond our present circumstances.

The expression of beauty has deep meaning. The expression of beauty is the ability to tune-in with the Cosmic Symphony which is the Plan and Purpose of all manifestation and of all life-forms in the universe. Thus, through the expression of beauty, we establish contact with those energies that secure our survival upon higher and higher levels of existence.

Culture is the manifestation of the will-to-survive and of the will-to-contact the Highest Beauty within the heart of the Living Fire in man and in cosmos.

The new age is the person. If the person is new, the age is new. Everything is new around him. The manifestation of the new age is the manifestation of one's higher Self. Culture is the collective manifestation of the true Selves of the people. That is how an *age* becomes *new*. Any regular and steady contact or experience with the higher Self manifests as culture, whether it is in a person or in masses of people. No one can enter into the new age unless he first enters into his intuitional plane, which reveals to him that the Greater Self is passing through the same experience on higher levels of existence. This understanding reveals that new cycles and new ages are opening for Him. These cycles and these new ages are opportunities for us to contact our intuitional plane, or the true Self, to also make that age or cycle a new age, a new cycle for us.

If a new cycle begins and you are not ready to understand and translate it through your life and relationship, the old age will continue for you, and you will be an obstacle on the path of those who are in the new age, who are the builders of the new age, and are the new age itself.

Everyday becomes a new day for the person who continuously expands his consciousness and sees things that he has never seen before, and responds to these new things in a way he never did before.

Culture is the manifestation of the Inner Beauty in man and in humanity. The Inner Beauty is only reached when we refine ourselves spiritually, mentally, emotionally, and physically. We need new transfigured vehicles to reach higher states of consciousness or awareness and to be able to express them and to live them creatively. It is only through such refinement that we can touch the beauty existing in man and in cosmos. When this beauty is manifested we have culture, which is the response of the human heart to beauty—to the creative fire.

Thus, culture becomes a bridge that leads from chaos to beauty, from darkness to light . . . Culture cannot be created by materialistic, competitive or fighting forces—not with vanities, hatred or war, but by touching the higher levels of spiritual achievements.

It is the achievement, the transformation of our nature, that expresses itself through our painting, music, literature, sculpture, architecture, craft, dance, morals, right-human-relations, and visions manifested through all human endeavors. Culture is the rainbow of peace between heaven and earth.

Culture is the result of experience; not the result of information. It is an expression of a level of being, a level of a new transmutation within, and not the result of the accumulation of knowledge.

A new age person is one who has fiery experiences with the higher levels of existence. Because of these fiery experiences he is highly fiery or cultured, and with all his being strives toward the Central Core of the fire. He expresses this fire of light, love, and power in his daily life and communications. A cultured person is the true expression of his Soul-nature—of his Spiritual and Divine nature. When the ancients spoke about the alchemical fire, the transmuting fire, they were referring to the fire in man.

The first real fire within a person is the transpersonal Self, or Solar Angel. The esoteric tradition says that these beings were once upon a time human beings and strove so hard and so long that eventually they released their Fiery Essence and became Fiery Beings or Shining Selves. They inspire man with great beauty and great love.

The next realm of fire in a person is called the Spiritual Triad, from whence stream forth abstract ideas—the Plan, joy, bliss, and direction. When a person's consciousness enters into such a field of fire, he becomes an Agni Yogi, or a person of synthesis, of compassion and understanding. The expressions of such a cultured person will be in higher beauty, in all fields of human endeavor.

The next field of fire is the Self, the Real Core in the phenomena called man. In this fire one becomes totally radioactive and Divine.

In the first fire you have creativity of talents. In the second fire you have the creativity of genius. In the third fire the result is higher: a person becomes Beauty Itself—the Savior—the Light of the world. One becomes as Buddha is, as Krishna is, as Christ is.

Culture is the path of evolution and transmutation, the resurrection of consciousness, making it all embracing, all inclusive.

Evolution produces better forms so that there can be greater contacts with the universe, and so that these contacts can be expressed in creative manifestation.

Transmutation occurs when the extinguished fire in the charcoal of the personality catches fire and burns brightly as a blazing flame.

Resurrection is the ability to withdraw our spirit from personal, group, self-oriented, or separative activities and lift it toward the Purpose of Life, the Purpose hidden in the Core of the Sun.

In new age education we will first emphasize the responsibility of evolving, transmuting, and resurrecting our nature. Without such a transformation all our knowledge can be used for self-destruction. A person without culture becomes an instrument of destruction and corruption.

When sages talked about tamas, rajas, and sattva in old Hindu literature, they referred to the three different conditions or states of the physical body; to the three different states of the emotional body; and to the three different states of the mental body.

—Inertia or tamas, is the condition of a piece of wood placed on the ground.
—Motion or rajas, is the state of the wood which catches fire and now is smoking.

—Rhythm or sattva, is the condition of that wood when the wood is changing into bright radioactive fire.

The same thing happens to our physical, emotional, and mental atoms. We have atoms in all our various bodies or vehicles that are in a state of inertia, but when fire from higher realms descends it makes these atoms active, and eventually radioactive and rhythmic.

When the physical body becomes totally sattvic the body is in a state of transfiguration, because no impurity exists in the body when the spiritual fire infuses it.

When the emotional body becomes totally sattvic there is a state of transfiguration, and the person turns into a fountain of peace, love and magnetism, because the spiritual fire purifies it to such a degree that all glamors are almost evaporated from its domain.

When the mental body is totally sattvic there is then the enlightened person, and this person with his complete physical, emotional, and mental nature passes through the third Initiation, or into the state of total transfiguration in time and space.

The fire from the Inner Core of a person is called psychic energy. If a person is charged with his own psychic energy, or with the psychic energy of the Hierarchy and Christ, or Shamballa, he will be a leader, peacemaker and illuminator. All problms in our personality and social lives are the result of the absence of such a fire of psychic energy.

Psychic energy is fire released from the Solar Angel, Spiritual Triad, or from the Inner Core—the Self.

Every time the atoms of our vehicles or the vehicles themselves are in the process of becoming sattvic, they present complicated problems as they pass the middle state, which is the rajasic state—the state of motion. It is here that people need great help in order to make their transition from motion to rhythm. Of greatest help for them is contact with culture. Culture opens for them the path to the domain of harmony and rhythm.

Most of our problems in life result from our inertia, glamors, and illusions. The Inner Fire wipes away this inertia, and the physical body becomes the instrument of the Soul. When fire touches the emotional body it gradually cleans the glamors, and the emotional body then becomes the purified matter of intuition. That is what the destruction of the emotional body means. When the glamors are cleared away one is full of positive emotions. In such a condition the emotional body reflects the intuitional fire. One keeps the power of sensitivity, but rejects any touchiness, glamor, attachment, upheaval, self pity, or depression.

The transformation of the mind now starts—which is the purification of the mind from illusions. Many obstructions from past lives, or thoughtforms of others hang around us as fears or crystallized thoughtforms. These slowly disappear because the fire burns them and the pure substance of mind remains. This reflects the power of the Will.

When all of these are achieved by a person he is truly a cultured person, a creative person, a person of vision, and a person of bliss and power. Culture is a progressive transmutation into the Fire of Light—into the Fire of Love and Power, as symbolized in the Transfiguration Initiation of Jesus.

It was significant that Jesus took three of His disciples to a mountain. This means He took His three vehicles of expression to a very high state of consciousness and transfigured them. When they saw that Jesus turned into a blazing light, the three disciples fell on their knees and put their foreheads on the ground in a supreme act of worship.

The three disciples symbolize the three vehicles of Jesus, which were transformed in the light of Inner Divinity. The three vehicles of Jesus became totally sattvic, pure fire, and expressed the Inner Radiance. This was the first major Initiation through which all of us one day will pass providing we strive, work hard, and serve humanity.

Thus, culture is a progressive entrance into greater fire, into greater Light, Love and Power, and the manifestation of such progress through all human endeavors.

A cultured person creates the culture of races and opens a path of resurrection for them. Take away the great labors of the cultural people on this planet, and only dullness and crime will remain.

Culture always remains, because culture is our state of beingness, and we never lose it. Culture is what *great*:

—politicians gave us as the science of rulership and leadership;
—educators gave us as the science of expanding our consciousness;
—philosophers gave us as the science of ideas;

—artists gave us as the science of sublimation and ecstasy;
—scientists gave us as systemized knowledge so that we will know ourselves and the universe better;
—religions gave us as the science of communication with the Almighty Power;
—modern economists gave us as the science of handling the energy of money and matter. It is also why we have sacred ceremonies and rituals.

These are all parts of culture, and the heritage of the ages. Without them our earth would be a dead moon.

I received some bookmarks on which are written the words of the great artist, Nicholas Roerich. They say:

"Peace through *Culture."*

This is a profound statement. There is no peace without culture, because peace is the manifestation of the highest within us, throughout our life.

Roerich once said, "Culture is the reverence of light. Culture is love of humanity; culture is fragrance, the unity of life and beauty. Culture is the synthesis of uplifting and sensitive attainments. Culture is the armor of light. Culture is salvation. Culture is the motivating power. Culture is the Heart."[15]

The seven great fields of human endeavor are created by the influence of seven types of energy, which in esoteric literature are called the seven Rays.

Culture can be expressed through the seven great fields of human endeavor. For example, we have great statesmen, great lawmakers, people of great decisions and leadership. All these people create a part of great culture in the political field.

Culture is created when a first ray person contacts his head center or a first ray group contacts its head center; and through the head center enters into the realm of laws and principles. In the very early ages of history we had great lawmakers, great leaders, who gave us the basic laws of right-human-relationships and created a great culture.

Second ray culture is the education of the refinement of the vehicles and expansion of consciousness, which comes from the heart center, from the Hierarchy. The second field of endeavor created a marvelous educational system all over the world with its institutions.

The third ray culture is the result of the mental and abstract analysis of things and events to find out the essence and the cause. A great culture on this ray arose in Greece and Egypt, and scattered all over the world. People on this ray try to find the meaning behind the phenomena, the Purpose behind the form—any form, and the Plan hidden in chaos. The throat center is mostly used in this activity.

The fourth ray culture is the result of the endeavor to express the divine harmony, and beauty and rhythm through sound, through movement, through color, and through form. This endeavor resulted in the masterpieces of the world; in literature, sculpture, architecture, music, painting, drama, and dance. Without the labor of the fourth ray, humanity's life would indeed be dry. This ray primarily uses the throat, heart, and head centers.

The fifth ray culture is the result of our endeavor to penetrate into the nature of the physical, emotional, and mental realms in an effort to find the laws of these planes of existence and to help human beings live a more conscious life, a life that aids their evolution. We have such a culture in medicine and in all branches of scientific endeavor. Scientists are builders of culture because they are revealing the inner laws, the principles, and the Plan.

The sixth ray culture is the result of our endeavor to aspire, admire, transform, and initiate through ideas or ideals. Ideas are fiery waves of energy. It is through such flaming ideas that man can conquer the unconquerable. That is what the religions gave us and will continue to contribute in the future. The sixth ray endeavor gave us all the culture related to all religions.

The seventh ray culture is the result of an endeavor to relate spirit with matter, and to make the spirit manifest itself through the form, in higher and higher spirals. This ray gave us all rituals and ceremonies of the world. Ritual and ceremony are formed by those rhythms, colors, sounds, and forms that in their totality will draw spirit into action and then into birth. Rituals and ceremonies, if they are genuine, are formulas through which the energy flows and brings changes in matter, emotions, and thoughts.

Finance and economics are related to a subtle energy, which seventh ray people try to control, manipulate, or use constructively in the form of money and its equivalent. Money is energy which will be used for the manifestations of subjective beauty.

In these seven ray endeavors the creative fire expresses itself, and the totality of this expression is called the world of culture or the gradual expression of the inner resources of light, love, and power.

A great Sage says in his book,

"Certainly, the evolution of the Spirit requires refinement, without which it is impossible to build. Each one who considers himself a server of Culture must accept the affirmation of the manifested synthesis, for how are the steps of Culture to be built without a cautious attitude? Therefore, each foundation must be guarded for affirmation to the world. Culture is built not with an attitude of coarseness towards the subtle energies and thought, but by a creative attitude of caution and responsibility. Hence, while constructing, one should remember about refinement and about striving to the higher spheres. Thus the evolution of the spirit is reached."[16]

All creative people on all rays must remember their responsibility: to create in harmony with divine intent, in harmony with the highest good for humanity. That is why one needs refinement, and needs to be cautious. When you create, you release fire. Fire can build or destroy, lead or mislead. This is why a great responsibility is placed upon the shoulders of all creative people so that their creation is not activated by the motive of exploitation, distortion, and destruction.

Responsibility emphasizes striving and no one can keep himself in the right line of creativity if his life is not a continuous path of striving and refinement. Striving is the effort to contact the highest within us, and the endeavor to express it as purely as possible. Striving is the process of charging your nature with psychic energy and uplifting your nature to greater harmony with the divine intent. It is through such striving that unity with your true Self is reached and the inner harmony is established.

A great Sage says, ". . . It may be pointed out that the first sign of Culture is the absence of personal discords."[17]

Chapter 4

CULTURE AND CO-MEASUREMENT

ULTURE IS CLOSELY RELATED to co-measurement. There is no culture without co-measurement. We can even say that the culture of a nation is the collective expression of the degree of its co-measurement.

Culture is the harmonious combination of all factors which condition the ability to create, to love, to communicate, to understand, and to live a more abundant life.

Co-measurement is the ability to take into consideration all those factors that are related to the act you intend to perform.

Co-measurement is like composing a symphony in which every note you write will add to the total harmony of your music and vision.

Co-measurement creates synthesis in any field of human endeavor. In painting, co-measurement is the ability to choose each color in such a way and with such an intensity that the painting as a whole presents your vision and imparts to others your inspiration.

Co-measurement is like creating a dance in which every movement you make will be in accord with the whole dance, even if you make additions to it.

A man who is endowed with co-measurement does not act, speak or write without taking into consideration as many factors as possible which are related to his actions, speech, or writings. A modern example of this is the architect who prepares the blueprints of a house taking into full consideration the rules and regulations of the building, health, fire, environmental, and other departments.

The deeper spiritual meaning may be to live a life which is "affirmed" by the plan and dedicated to the welfare of humanity.

Co-measurement enables you to create harmonious relationships between your acts, motives, the plan, the purpose, and the need of humanity. A surfer is a beautiful example of co-measurement: he keeps his balance and uses the waves and his movements in harmony with the surf.

You cannot use co-measurement in your relationships if you do not have pure sensitivity or intuitive perception about the physical, emotional, mental, and spiritual conditions of those with whom you are related.

Co-measurement does not exist if you do not have a standard measure within yourself. The standard measure can be your direct spiritual contact with the Plan and with the Purpose.

Co-measurement also means to look at a problem or object through the eyes of those who are looking at the object—before you look at it.

Co-measurement is to measure all possibilities and all detriments before one starts organizing an activity.

Co-measurement is needed also when one is selecting co-workers. Their background, their present effort in their education, their future possibilities, their possible failures, and their qualifications in regard to the job is closely considered.

Co-measurement also can be seen in creative action, in which all components have been selected in proportionate dosage and related to those psychological levels and moods for which they are presented to secure maximum effectiveness.

Co-measurement can be applied also to one's own attire, conversation, and behavior. Co-measurement is based on discrimination, selection, choice, sense of relationship, harmony, ability to evaluate, and true insight.

Co-measurement applies also to the relationship of subjective and objective considerations. When one is acting on the subjective level and in the meantime adjusting his action with the subjective laws, principles and virtues, he is applying co-measurement. It is also true that a man dealing with subjective values must take into consideration the objective consequences and effects of his subjective undertaking.

Co-measurement leads a man, a group or a nation to unity and synthesis. It evokes respect, gratitude, and a sense of responsibility.

Co-measurement needs a well-developed mind, intuitive insight and lots of knowledge in various fields. As the mind of a man develops, as his intuitive faculty unfolds, and as his field of knowledge increases he can better use co-measurement, provided that he has a deep sense of unity. You can see co-measurement in high level political leadership. A leader must consider all the fields of human endeavor before he makes decisions and gives orders. His success depends on his co-measurement. Co-measurement means to select those factors which will support each other in a given direction.

Co-measurement is a panoramic view without losing the details of the field.

I had a teacher who was a mechanical engineer. We used to work in a railway depot. Every time an engine needed repair, he used to listen carefully to all the noises of the engine and then give his diagnosis. He was always right. Once, when I asked him how he was always so successful in his diagnosis, he answered that it is easy if you try to hear all the noises of the engine and slowly concentrate on noises that do not fall into the harmony of the noises of the other parts. This is co-measurement.

We can use co-measurement in almost all of our actions. It is an expanding focus in an ever-changing field of action.

Co-measurement unfolds and grows as our capacity to use our logic and reasoning develops.

"It is right to remember that work with Us has but a single direction—that of co-measurement and goal-fitness. The traitor of the path is simply bereft of these qualities, and his fate is as that of a kitten at sea."[1]

"It is essential not to fear to broaden your activity, because this is the best way to co-measurement. Sitting under one tree, one may presume that it is the center of the world. But disseminating the substance of spirit through the entire world, we become as fire, all-pervading."[2]

Love and compassion are the foundations of co-measurement. Love is inclusive, compassion is all-inclusive, and it is inclusiveness which allows a man to act with co-measurement. Love and compassion open all fields, all dimensions and if the consciousness is pure and expanding, then a man has the ability to co-measure all that he does.

The beauty of creation is that every part is related to the rest. Nothing is created without the support of everything else—just like a cosmic IBM machine in which all the parts of cosmos are related to each other and support each other and also exist because of each other.

Co-measurement is the path leading to expansion, towards Infinity, creating synthesis on each spiral on the path of perfection.

A great Sage says, "Loss of co-measurement is loss of the path."[3]

The greatest politician is the one who has the highest co-measurement. For him there is one interrelated world, and his plans, decisions, and actions are the result of his consideration of this interrelationship.

Co-measurement inspires a man to be extremely careful in his judgment of others. Co-measurement often seals the lips and leads a man into silence.

Co-measurement also sustains the spirit of patience.

Co-measurement must control not only what you do, but also what you do not do. Co-measurement must control not only our speech, but our silence as well.

The absence of co-measurement is the cause of failure.

Co-measurement is a phenomena of harmony. But harmony can be achieved only on the foundation of a tuning-fork, on the foundation of a keynote. This keynote or this principle is the intuitive realization that Life is seeking to improve the process of perfection through sacrificial service. The fulfillment of this principle is the goal of co-measurement.

Co-measurement cannot start and operate without the above said principle, although this principle is not always on the surface of the consciousness, but is deep in our being and from that depth it controls the process of co-measurement.

No Brotherhood or true Ashram exists without co-measurement. A leader is greater if he has greater ability in co-measurement. A brother is greater when he acts by co-measurement. All brothers are related to each other through co-measurement. Co-measurement makes them free, and makes them responsible to each other. Only co-measurement can build the bridge between freedom and responsibility.

Equilibrium, balance, and harmony can be created only by co-measurement.

Co-measurement is the mathematics of the universe by which it creates.

Through co-measurement one can express the rhythm of his own soul, then through greater co-measurement he expresses the rhythm of his Master and Ashram.

In greater co-measurement he expresses the rhythm of the Hierarchy and Shamballa. Co-measurement is the ability to harmonize one's own life with greater and greater centers.

Beauty, solemnity, and gratitude cannot exist without co-measurement.

Great leaders, great creative people are those people who throughout ages exercised co-measurement in all their strivings and creative endeavors.

How to develop co-measurement?

EXERCISE ONE

Choose an object such as a pencil, paper, chair, table, or lamp and try to find all of the possible stages the object passed through to become what it now is. Do this for one month. Then try to imagine the various usages of the object you considered. Do this for one month. The third month try to find the ways you yourself used the object.

After three months you will see a considerable change in your consciousness. You will have a broader scope of thinking, and a greater ability to relate and adapt.

After three months you can choose an abstract subject, such as beauty, solemnity, responsibility, and do the same thing as you did with your concrete subject.

Thus, try to find in your meditation how these words, these ideas came into being; how they originated and how they developed. You don't need to look in an encyclopedia to find your answers. They are right within your Soul, bring them out.

In the second month try to see the various ways in which these concepts, ideas, words were used.

In the third month try to find out the ways you used these concepts in your creative and practical life.

In the next three months you can take a very abstract subject such as *motion*, and try to find the relationship of motion to the motion of various objects, in your body, in your city, on the planet, solar system and beyond and try to find a relationship between all of these motions or movements.

Through such exercises you prepare yourself not only for executive positions but also for higher leadership. People think that positions can be grasped by artificial means. This is possible but it brings many disadvantages with it. Rightful positions come to those who are ready for them. When you are ready, your position will not be a burden for you or an occasion of failure, but a cycle of great joy, spiritual service, and satisfaction. Co-measurement is an ever-expanding relationship.

EXERCISE TWO

There is another exercise which can be done individually or in group formation. This exercise is called *questioning*.

A group can sit together and choose a subject. Then the members ask you questions from various viewpoints. For example, *Harmlessness*—the questions you might be asked may be from a political, educational, philosophical, artistic, scientific, religious, or economic viewpoint and you will try to answer as best you can. Such an exercise discloses all your weaknesses and brings you to the realization where you stand regarding that particular subject. This gives you a chance to try and expand the field of your information, to cultivate greater ability to think and formulate and see your object from as many viewpoints as possible. Such an exercise cultivates the faculty of co-measurement.

Try to be considerate in all your thoughts, emotions, and actions. This is a life-long exercise through which you prevent misfortune on your path, and minimize your karma. Be considerate when you talk or when you keep silence. By using consideration you will penetrate into the psychology of yourself and others. You will balance energies and forces, and eventually develop a true spirit of co-measurement, and become a man of culture within your heart.

In co-measurement, advanced disciples and initiates adapt their level to the level of their co-workers and environment. They may even delay their graduation or initiation so as not to release certain energies to their environment, energies which can be destructive.

A disciple does not take initiation because he wants it but because he forgets all about it in his sacrificial service.

A group that is integrated and rendering a great service in greater fields is a group that is developing deeper layers of co-measureemnt.

A failing group is a group which does not exercise co-measurement. Groups go toward internal and outer disintegration because of lack of co-measurement.

Responsibility is based on co-measurement. When you remove a stone from a wall that is connected with most of the other stones, you are destroying the building. Before you remove it you must know what that stone is related to. One can exercise his sense of responsibility only through co-measurement.

Those who criticize or flatter people have lack of co-measurement. They criticize because they are stuck with a characteristic of another person which they don't like; or they flatter someone if they think that flattery will help them obtain their self-interests. Co-measurement does not allow the parts to cover the whole.

Co-measurement is related also to time. Sometimes it causes fast and drastic action, and sometimes it causes non-action. It's goal is neither action nor non-action, but to restore equilibrium, or create harmonious development.

Take an act that you performed and examine it: why did you do it; how did you do it; what factors contributed to it; what factors were opposing it; what kind of influences preconditioned your action? Thus, keeping your act at the center you find many factors related to it—such an expanding field in your consciousness develops co-measurement.

Co-measurement is a conscious selection of those factors or

actions which contribute to your success, to the achievement of your goal.

When a man is blindly following his urges and drives and is conducting his life in the sleep state, he will be the victim of changes around him. The outer world will control his life and use his life.

Co-measurement releases him from such slavery because of his selective activity. Discriminative selection not only leads you toward co-measurement, but also liberates you from a mechanically conducted life.

Co-measurement is a steady progress into greater and greater fields of relationships. It may start with your personal life, then expand into your family, national, and international life; and it may even go into solar, galactic, and cosmic life.

Initiations, or expansions of consciousness, are the result of the ever expanding ability of co-measurement.

Co-measurement starts with being *considerate* or being circumspect.

Exams in our schools or universities are the tests of our mental co-measurement. Geometry, algebra, are great tests for co-measurement in those fields.

Co-measurement is supported by intuition and intellect. Intuition synchronizes your direction with the subtle and subjective principles, and intellect adjusts your life in the three lower worlds according to the impressions it receives through the intuition. This is how co-measurement advances—penetration, impression, and appropriation.

Co-measurement advances when your sense of evaluation begins to develop. When you strive to higher values you need a higher level of co-measurement.

Co-measurement always reveals higher values and leads to things that are relatively more permanent, eternal, or infinite. Thus if you are choosing things that are good for your body but not good for your soul, you are not making the right choice. The wrong choice will not allow you to develop co-measurement.

Co-measurement leads to higher and eternal or infinite values. Co-measurement is based on the laws and principles of cosmos.

In co-measurement you are taking your stand within the Soul, within the Spiritual Triad, within the Ashram, and are directing your life from such an elevated level.

Every time you are bothered by your conscience, it is because you were short in co-measurement.

Co-measurement brings increasing joy and success. When a man stands on the border of intuition and intellect and uses co-measurement, wisdom dawns in his mind. Wisdom is the flower of co-measurement. After wisdom is gained, all actions of man spring out from the spirit of co-measurement.

Chapter 5

LOVE ENERGY

I

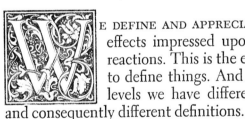E DEFINE AND APPRECIATE things according to the effects impressed upon us, and according to our reactions. This is the easiest way for human beings to define things. And because we are on different levels we have different reactions and responses, and consequently different definitions.

Love is one of those realities which we define and appreciate because of its results.

If it makes us happy, we say love is good.

If it makes us safe, we say love is a protection.

If it makes us miserable, deprived or sick, love is something that must be refused.

If love brings us money, love is good.

If love takes all our money, love is not good.

Thus, we always judge love because of its effects, not because of what in reality it is.

109

Customarily we have two ways of knowing love:

1. Through its effects; or by using it.
2. Through identification with it; or through being it.

But if you truly want to know something, you must *be it*. For instance, if you really want to know what love is, you must be love. You can use love, but in using love you are judging it through what it does. However, by being it you really know what it is.

When you use love energy and try to know it through analysis, through its effects, or through your reactions and responses, you will not know it. The only way to know what love really is, is *to be* love.

We are told that God is Love, and that we are seeds of God scattered in space. All that proceeded from Him is crystallized love— all manifestation is tangible love.

If a man or any living being or form wants to go back to the Source, there is only one way—to be a living love. No matter on what plane love operates, it produces or creates forms to further the evolution of the spirit.

There are seven levels of expression of love:

1. The first expression of love is *sex* which can be translated as: attraction, cohesion, affinity, understanding, or fusion on different levels.

It can be physical sex, in human or lower kingdoms.

It can be emotional sex, some kind of affinity which is not necessarily related to physical sex. You love someone, you love your country, or group, or nation, and in such a love there is no sex. In this stage, instead of thinking only of your pleasure, you think of the pleasure of others.

Then we have mental sex. You may love a beauty, a talent, a creative person, and become inspired and create many poems or art works. Dante's "Divine Comedy" is the result of mental love.

Also, you may not even have any physical or emotional interest in a person but love his ideas, his visions, and they produce creative activities in your mind.

Sometimes to have a higher level expression of love, one may even turn off his physical and emotional loves. Many great visions, ideas, projects, and plans are created when two or more people put their minds together and inspire each other, as a mental-level sex activity. In all these cases, one person acts as a positive pole, another person acts as a negative pole, and the friction between these poles creates physical, emotional, or mental forms.

Love is sex, and sex is love. Sex is the energy which relates matter and spirit, and when spirit and matter come together we have the manifested universe with all its forms. Thus love is in a process of expression, radioactivity, or in a process of revelation. Love reveals.

As we love more, we become more love. If we love only physically, we are ten percent love. When we add to it emotional love, we become twenty percent love. When we add to it mental love, we become thirty percent love. As we truly love, we increase in being love. As we proceed to higher degrees of loving, our field of contact and the intensity of our joy increases.

Man is a drop of fiery love fallen into matter. Our responsibility is to release ourselves and bloom in all dimensions. As we become more love, we understand better what love is. We may listen to many lectures or read books about love, but it does not help us until we start becoming love.

All manifestation of love on any plane is beautiful if it serves the Divine Plan.

Sex exists on all planes. For some, sex is a painful memory. For them it is syphilis, gonorrhea, abortion, divorce, crime, misery; but all these in reality are the results of the misuse of love energy and cannot be the real definitions of love. The real definition is related to our mechanism and its reactions to love energy.

2. The second expression of love is *goodwill.* You will good for others. To will good for others means to meet their needs, and prepare them in a way that they eventually meet their own need and the needs of others. Without this second step, goodwill turns into selfish interests.

Think good for others. Any time any negative thought or image comes into your mind reject it, and in its place immediately express a positive thought.

Do the same with your feelings. Any time a negative thought or image comes into your emotional nature, replace it with a loving feeling.

Also, if you are ready to take an action which is harmful, criminal, or destructive, immediately stop and reverse it. Express a positive, benevolent action toward the one against whom you were ready to take harmful action. In this way you release that love energy, and eventually feel that you are love itself. And because you are love, you can only love and will good to others.

Changing and reversing the course of action of your mind, emotions, and physical body is not easy of course. But through effort you can learn how to do it.

When I used to do naughty things as a child, my mother would say to me, "I hope you live a long life to realize how much you need to improve yourself." This was said instead of a curse. Another time she would say, "May God give you health so that you can earn money with your own labor and learn to appreciate its value." She would also say, "May you have lots of children so that you will know what it means to be a parent."

Thus, instead of wishing or doing something negative, you can find a positive expression even in a tempting situation.

In goodwill, you must also develop your ability of discrimination so that you check your thoughts, feelings, and actions before they are expressed by you.

It is your transformation that can cause transformation in others. A man of goodwill *is* a greater *love*, and this love evokes love in others, and leads them to actions of goodwill.

It seems to me that the first tangible expression of love is goodwill. If you do not will good to others, you do not have love, even if you write books about it.

Goodwill is the first step out of the unconscious and mechanical urge which we call sex. Goodwill is the first step of conscious usage of love energy.

The whole purpose and process of evolution is to elevate you and to bring you back to your original state of being—which you had as a Divine Essence before identifying with matter—together with all that you have learned on your return journey Home.

Your original state of being was love, and you are going back again to become pure love, and the only way to be love is to love.

Wherever we fail on the path of love, there we produce delay and suffering and act against our own destiny.

As you expand the actions of your goodwill, you become more love, and you become a man of goodwill, doing things that are good for others. Goodwill always tries to meet a need. It does not take, but gives.

When a person of goodwill tries to meet the need of other people, he does not seek self gratification, but only the pleasure of those he tries to help.

In goodwill no one compensates you for what you did for others, but you do grow in love. That is the non-expected reward. And that is the greatest reward, because there is no higher reward than the awareness that you are getting closer to your destiny—becoming more love.

3. The third expression of love in the human kingdom is *right human relationship*. This is love energy functioning on the higher mental planes, or on transpersonal levels. When a man relates himself as a soul to another soul, he creates a right human relationship. No one can create right human relationship as long as he relates to people from the level of his personality interests. It is only Soul level contact that makes the personality act in the path of right human relationship. Relationship on Soul levels is relationship based on harmlessness, selflessness, and clear vision.

Right human relationship cannot be created in any family, in any group, nation or humanity until the parts of the greater whole begin to communicate with each other on the Soul level, with Soul interest and vision. Of course the personality is involved in this action, but it is not the controlling factor, only an instrument.

Only the Soul knows what *right* is because It is in contact with the Plan and the Purpose of the Great Planetary Life and your life. Your mind does not know what right and wrong are except when enlightened by the Soul. Your mind rationalizes and finds many excuses for your actions, even if you know in your heart that those actions were wrong.

Right human relationship is to live in such a way that you let the beauty of other human beings shine out. First you recognize their beauty, even if that beauty is a little jewel hidden under a pile of rubbish, then you create right conditions for that jewel to shine out with its full beauty.

The greater your love is, the greater detachment you will have from the "personality" lives of others. The more love you have, the more creative you will be.

Greater love helps you endure the pain of the present caused by your past deeds. Greater love maks you tolerant and forgiving of the acts of human beings who consciously or unconsciously try to hurt you.

Right human relationship is based on the fact that all human beings are divine in their Essence and you relate with them to help them live in the Light of their own Divinity. Right human relationship means to make violence and self-destructive activities impossible through acts of peace, renunciation, spiritual education, and through the sense of righteousness.

It is important to realize that until you function in the light of the Soul, you cannot create right relationship within your own physical, emotional, and mental systems. And those who do not have right relationships within themselves are those people who distort right human relationships in every contact they make.

Problems in humanity, or in any person or group, can be solved if that person, group, or humanity raises its level and looks down on the problem from the Soul level.

Soul consciousness takes you out of your personality problems, and yo·ı look down upon the petty matters in which you were involved Once you see them, your problems start to dissolve.

When we try to show another human being how ugly, short, unwise or unsuccessful he is, he hates us and tries to belittle us, to prove that we are not better than he is. But when you see his beauty, he realizes his own shortcomings and silently improves himself, and respects your beauty because you raised him up to the level of beauty.

The hindrances to right human relationships are five in number:

a. Imposition of one's own will on others
b. Greed
c. Unrighteousness
d. Uncooperativeness
e. Pride

If we really overcome these five destructive forces, we will raise our consciousness to the Soul level and not be caught in activities that are against right human relations.

a. When you *impose your will* on others, you are making right human relationship impossible. Right human relationship is not the result of obeying some will imposed upon us, but is the outcome of self-realization, understanding, and Soul-consciousness. To the degree that you impose your will upon others, you are retarding the progress of their unfoldment and hindering the possibility of right human relations. When you are preventing someone from reaching the level where he can exercise right human relations, you are delaying your own growth and progress on the path of love energy.

Imposition of your will may take many forms. You can impose yourself by your physical force, money, power, position, fear, bribery, flattery. In whatever way you try to impose yourself, you are standing against right human relations.

This can apply to groups and nations too. To create right human relations we must leave other groups and nations free in their religious and political ideas, and not try to impose our views on them.

If you have something beautiful, you must not force others to admit its beauty, but you must educate and raise their consciousness in such a way that they see the beauty through their own efforts. Then they can admit the beauty and enjoy it.

Imposition creates rejection and fanaticism, and right human relationships cannot be established in a condition where people are rejecting, and where people try to impose themselves. Imposition creates slaves, and slaves never understand what right human relationship is, because slavery acts without a sense of proportion.

b. *Greed.* Whether it is the greed of a man, of a group, or of a nation, it is a great obstacle on the path of right human relations. In greed one makes himself the center of the universe and uses others to feed his glamor. In the ancient world greed was symbolized by a barrel without a bottom. You can never fill such a barrel. It is an unsatisfied thirst for material possessions, which makes one find many ways and means to exploit others, to try to fill the empty barrel.

It was greed that destroyed the great empires of ancient history, and it is greed that makes our joy and beauty dry up. Imagine Alexander the Great driven by unsatisfied greed to conquer the world. After his death all of his empire fell apart.

Greed eventually dulls the sensitivity of the human soul, and the cycle of unhappiness begins. No one can contribute to the great labor of right human relations if he is caught by the glamor of greed. A man of greed is a danger to his family, nation, humanity, and to himself.

I was talking with a millionaire. "You have money. What if you help us to build a beautiful Ashram with modern facilities?"

"You know," he answered, "I did not come to talk about money. I came to tell you something very important that is bothering me."

"What is it?"

"I am not happy."

"How did it start?"

"I do not know. Year after year, as I made more money, more business, my joy and peace of mind disappeared, and with increasing income my fear and anxieties increased. There must be something wrong with me but I can't find it."

"You already know it," I said, "because when I put my finger upon your wound, you did not like it."

"What wound are you talking about?"

"I asked if you would contribute money to us, and you immediately replied, 'I did not come to talk about money.' The greed for money is your wound, is your problem. That is why you reacted immediately. If you really want to regain your joy and peace, use your accumulated money to create right human relations, more education, more health."

He smiled and said, "I know, you are telling me all of this to make me give you money."

To cure onself from the glamor of greed one must pour forth love, must be giving and cooperating with those who are trying to build a new world based on right human relationship.

Right human relationship can be understood if one watches how a healthy body functions; all organs and systems are in right relationship with each other. Each of them works for the welfare of the body the best way they can, because their individual welfare depends upon the welfare of the whole body. If any organ or gland suddenly rebels and says it wants to work only for itself and not work for the whole body, you have a serious health problem.

Right human relationship is based on the idea that a man must live in a way that all the rest can profit from the life he lives, and because of the health of all the rest, he remains healthy.

All group, national, and international problems are the extensions of the problems of individuals. Cure the individual and you are paving the way for the health of nations and humanity.

c. The next hindrance is *unrighteousness*. This creates a real obstacle in international, group, and personal relationships.

A righteous person considers other human beings as himself. A righteous man lives in the presence of the Almighty Power, and cooperates with that Power.

Unrighteousness blocks the path of the life energy pouring into your system. It blocks the life energy of groups and nations. This means that unrighteousness is a way of committing suicide on an individual or national scale.

Most of the losses that we have had, most of the unpleasant accidents that we have experienced, are the reactions of the karmic laws to our past and present injustice. The law counterbalances our transgressions and we experience the pain of loss. Our laws on earth are a vague reflection of the greater laws of righteousness.

Righteousness is not only in our deeds, but is also in our thoughts and motives. Unless we catch unrighteous thoughts sneaking into our minds, we cannot act in a righteous way.

I know a man who had stolen some money from a dying person. Years later he was looking for a job and went to a company for an interview. He had the best qualifications among those who were applying for the job, but that day there was an accident on the freeway and he was two hours late for his appointment. When he finally came to the company, the employer refused to see him for he was two hours late.

This man told me his story and added, "I can't understand why I lost that job. But one thing comes into my mind. A few years ago I took some money that did not rightfully belong to me! Do you think that is why I lost this opportunity?"

It seems to me that the law functions in subtle ways and equalizes our balance sheet.

Criticism has been forbidden for ages because in criticism we are always unrighteous, since we look at things not from the viewpoint of others, but from the viewpoint of our interests.

Thus, unrighteousness disturbs right human relations.

d. The next obstacle is *uncooperativeness.*

Cooperation is the ability to see a common interest and the willingness to help others share in that common interest. Uncooperativeness lead to separatism and eventually to disintegration.

Through cooperation we step above our selfish interests and respect the interests of many. Through cooperation we understand each other, contact each other, and establish many communication lines which lead eventually to right human relations.

e. The fifth obstacle is *pride.*

Pride is a crystallized mentality in which one thinks that he is an object of worship and beauty, and the rest of the people are obliged to praise him every time he moves. Such a condition of mind eventually leads him into seclusion because his worshippers slowly disappear and he remains by himself.

Pride creates walls, and thus the energy flow of right human relations is hindered.

Pride does not allow him to see the value in others. Right human relationship grows and develops only in a consciousness which can see beauty, value, and merit in others.

4. The fourth expression of love is *service carried out in a great humanitarian project.*

The great Master Djwhal Khul says that, "A man . . . in service learns the power of love in its occult significance."[1]

In such service you are above your self, group, or national interest, and are now entering into the field of pure human interest, with your project having a global meaning.

People who are dedicated to such a service will see their love increasing to such a degree that they often will feel as one spirit in many bodies, and eventually they will feel that they are living as streams of love.

A young man says, "I love my girlfriend very much," and he marries her.

A few years later the love evaporates and you ask, "What happened?"

"We can't get along."

Or, you see an old man complaining, "She killed me for sixty years," and his wife says, "He made me live the life of a slave."

All these expressions indicate that these persons were the center of their universe. Once this center changes and becomes an interest for humanity as a whole, then the personality disagreements vanish. Then they cherish each other, even adore each other for the sake of a great service which they both enjoy. As they unite with the greater whole, they come closer to their Essence and become more love. You adore a man or woman when he or she is working for a great humanitarian project because such a work demands transformation, selflessness, culture, nobility, and spiritual integrity. As you serve you come closer to each other through trials, sacrifices, facing danger, and successes.

When a family or a group go beyond their average field of activity and dedicate themselves to a humanitarian project, you will see how the family or group members will become inseparable by the power of love which awakens them and fuses them.

I was talking with a mason who was cutting stones for a mosque in the Middle East. I asked, "Do you enjoy your job?"

"No, no, no," he said, "it is not a matter of enjoyment, it is a great responsibility to share in building a Temple for the Almighty One."

I was surprised that such a poor looking mason gave such a deep answer. I visited with him for many days and I found out from his friends that he was the chief of a great mystic organization, and had come to that place with his exceptional talent of masonry to *serve* a common project, which did not need lectures, but labor.

I also met a Russian who was collecting all of the Blavatsky writings and compiling them into a series of books. "Are they selling?" I asked.

"That is not the question in my mind," he answered. "The important thing is to make them available to the whole of humanity so that they see the deeper purpose of life, according to this great server."

Those of you who are very young, start building your vision for for a humanitarian service, and you will see how much your love will grow, your joy will grow. And in your old age you will not fall into the trap of depression and misery, for you will have so much to do for humanity that your personality situation will no longer bother you.

Every time you try to do something for humanity, you transform yourself into love, and tune in more with the divine harmony.

One day an old lady who was working day and night on a great humanitarian project forgot her appointment with the doctor. The doctor's secretary called her and said, "You missed your appointment."

"What appointment?"

"We were going to check your heart."

"But I don't have time to come."

"But, you may die if you do not cooperate with your doctor."

"I have no time this month, and I am not going to die because there are too many things that must be done."

It is often true that when you lose yourself in great service, you also lose your physical problems. Those people who worry too much about their health and death are those people who become sick more frequently and die early, and their short life is spent in worry.

When self-forgetful people meet, they immediately love each other because their love nature radiates out. As love goes deeper it needs a greater and higher mechanism to express itself.

Sex needs organs.

Goodwill needs heart and mind.

Right human relationship needs clear thinking with greater love.

Service for a humanitarian project needs Soul-consciousness and wisdom.

5. The fifth degree of expression of love can be defined as: *the vision of the future of humanity can be fulfilled through the divine Plan*, which indicates the way of survival, creativity, and manifestation of the beauty of mankind.

Working with the Plan brings us in contact with the higher substance of intuition by which the Plan is made, and there is more love energy in that substance than in the lower strata of the human constitution. This is a very intriguing point. As you function in a more subtle plane, your Essence radiates out more clearly, more abundantly. As you go higher, more love is available, because to go higher means to be more your own true Self.

When we come in contact with the intuitional plane, we touch that dimension of love which penetrates into all living forms in nature. Love on the intuitional plane changes into a supreme Light. That is why a person is illuminated or enlightened when he steps into that plane. It is on this plane that Light and Love become the same thing, and you now function as a person of wisdom. Wisdom not only sees the details but also reveals and synthesizes. Here again, you sense the unity with all living forms.

It is in this stage that man comes in contact with the LOVERS of humanity, the Masters of Wisdom. Master Djwhal Khul says, "When He (Christ) comes at the close of this century and makes His power felt, He will come as the Teacher of Love and Unity, and the keynote He will strike will be regeneration through love poured forth on all."[2]

6. The sixth expression of love is *contact with the Will of Shamballa.*

It is at this stage that love reveals to you the vision of the Purpose of life. You become a Lord of Compassion.

It is compassion that puts you in contact with the entire solar system, with the invisible lives in space, and the symphony of life expresses itself through you as a liberating power, and as an unconquerable will to sacrifice your life for the progress of life in the solar system.

7. The seventh expression of love is *the stage in which you become the embodiment of the Ray of Cosmic Love.*

A great Master says that in the history of humanity only Christ reached such a state of love, and He became the embodiment of the principle of Cosmic Love. That is why one of His great Disciples, M. M. says,

". . . My disciples must realize happiness in the love of Christ."[3]

It is in this degree of achievement that a man realizes himself as a stream of Cosmic Love, and becomes a radiant Son of God."

LOVE ENERGY

II

LOVE IS NOT A SENTIMENT. It is not an emotional attitude. It is the most powerful energy, the core of which is within the human being. Within each of us there is a fountain of great love which is blocked most of the time by our psychological disorders, negativity, distortions, vices, and ignorance.

Blocked love is a potential health hazard. It creates inner pressure, distraction of thought, and inhibits emotions and actions. When the stream of love is flowing, it nourishes the whole nervous system, the glands, and charges the whole man with enthusiasm, joy, and vitality. It also has an extremely powerful purifying influence on our threefold personality.

A truly loving man eventually turns into a cause of transformations. Whomever he touches he transforms. People change around him. They lose their negativity, grief, inertia, and become positive, joyful, rhythmic.

A loving man is a creative person. The love energy is creative energy. It brings out meaning, ideas, visions, and clothes them with expressions of beauty. A loving man opens the creative abilities in others. You become creative around a really loving man because he releases your Inner Core.

The progressive manifestation of love is nothing else but the progressive externalization or expression of the true Self within our form. Man in reality is naught else but a Spark of that Almighty Power, the nature of which is love.

Love has many dimensions and it expresses itself on many levels:

1. The first dimension of true love is *givingness*. A man likes to give. Giving for him is a joy and a great satisfaction. He gives objects, labor, smiles, time, wisdom, guidance, and money. He feels that nothing really belongs to him; he uses all that he has for the Plan and for the needs of others. Even when he accumu-

lates, he has in his mind to distribute it wisely, and meet the needs of those who otherwise are unable to meet their needs.

But the way he gives is controlled by intuitive discrimination. His giving does not paralyze other people, it does not create emotional reactions or greed in them, but leads them to the path of striving and giving. The reason for this is that as the love energy passes through their systems, it breaks crystallizations and attachments, and sets them free from the slavery of possessiveness.

A detached person is one who can see things as they are in their true relationships. When the number of such detached people increases in the world, you will see the elimination of such misery and possessiveness which have brought our planet to the abyss of destruction. Such possessiveness gives us manifold corruption, wars, exploitations, violations of human rights, and depletes the planet of its resources. In the last analysis the pollution of the planet is the result of human greed and possessiveness.

A giving person feels that the giver and the receiver are from the same essence, and he will not be complete if the other self does not receive. A selfish person is a man who puts both socks on one foot and none on the other foot. Lack of love reduces our power of reasoning, logic and understanding, and makes us channels of dark urges, drives, and glamors of the world.

A loving person has an understanding heart, and he puts his socks on both feet, because he knows that his two feet belong to one body, to one Soul, as all men belong to one super Soul. Such a person has the innate conviction that all human beings are manifestations of the One existence.

Such a person eventually finds out that the things that he keeps for his own are the things that he loses. The things that he gives away are the things that he receives and keeps. In giving we increase, in taking we decrease if in the meantime we do not follow the rule of giving.

A giving person gives not for his own interests, but for the interests of the receivers. Meeting a need in others is building a bridge in one's own consciousness and enriching the garden of one's own heart.

A giving person does not expect any recognition from the receiver. We can truly give if there is no expectation in our heart. Any expectation is a chain tied to the thing we gave to others, and it makes us very uncomfortable if we try to walk with someone while our feet are chained. It is the need of the other person that evokes in him the giving impulse.

A giving person knows also why he is giving; intuitively he feels the need, and he gives wisely so as not to lead the other person into inertia.

One must ask himself, "Am I a giving person? Am I interested in giving or taking? Do I feel that in giving I am truly receiving, and in receiving I am giving?"

Those people who are possessed by the things they have are greedy people, and greed is the opposite of love; it is also opposite to the true nature of a human being. In greed man actually distorts his own energy balance, and creates conflict in his system. He creates a short circuit in his communication system. Greed means to accumulate for his separated self. Love means to disperse values to others, because love understands, sees, and thinks in unity.

2. The second dimension of love is a life based on *beauty*. In this dimension man lives for beauty; he stands for beauty. Love makes everything beautiful. Love makes man see beauty, admire beauty, and be beauty.

A loving person sees the beauty of trees, flowers, rivers, the beauty of all nature, and he takes time to enjoy it. He feels that to enjoy beauty means to increase beauty and to be grateful for beauty. To admire beauty means to transform into beauty. Such a person inspires beauty in all his relationships, and because of that he increases love in the world.

As a person loves in the deeper sense and makes his love a radiant beauty, he gradually tunes in with the Symphony of the Universe. The Symphony of the Universe is composed of all laws, principles, energies, and manifestations which as a whole express a Cosmic Plan and a Cosmic Purpose. Through love a person tunes in with this Symphony, and as he gradually demonstrates in his life a deeper love, the Symphony Divine pours down through all of his expressions and actions as manifestations of beauty.

A life of creativity is the result of such a communion. All truly creative people are loving people, and people who are in tune with the Cosmic Symphony. Creativity is the ability to express this Symphony.

Again, we must remember that such a state of achievement does not come to us at once. It takes years and sometimes lives to reach such a dimension.

People have not yet seen the value of admiration. Admiration of beauty is a great release of love energy into space. This love energy purifies space.

Those who admire beauty in any form become more beautiful. Admiration is a transformation process in which man becomes that which he admires. Admiration is supreme receptivity of beauty. Once a person begins to admire his life, he enters into a path of transformation. Many psychological distortions can be cured in a moment of admiration and ecstasy.

Once the great artist, Nicholas Roerich, said, "Through beauty we conquer."

Beauty is within each human being. This is very important to realize. Once a person contacts his own Inner Beauty, the Divine Presence, the Divine Symphony within his inner being, he is not the same person. He is a blooming, unfolding flower. The release and expression of Inner Beauty can conquer a life of ugliness, ignorance, guilt, and disease. As the Inner Beauty unfolds itself, man conquers his nature and all that is not beautiful within his vehicles and their expressions.

3. The third dimension of love expresses itself as a *striving for the unity of mankind*. At this stage the person stands for total unity, and lives a unifying life. This is a challenging period because most of the people who are separative in their thinking and attitudes have their interests supported by enterprises based on a separative spirit. Such people do not tolerate men or women who truly stand for unity.

Most political parties in the world exist because they are separative. They see only their viewpoint and their interest. All religions are separative. That is why they exist as separate religions. Nations exist because they feel that they are different than others. And because people behind all these activities live in separative thinking, any person of unity stands dramatically opposite to their interests. That is why in all ages such people were martyred. But, it is very interesting to note that the best that humanity has in its culture and civilization is the gift of those people who thought, felt, and acted on the principle of unity.

For such people there is only one humanity, one world, one interest. They think that the separative spirit brought to humanity suffering, diseases, crimes, exploitations, violations of rights and destruction, and turned the planet into a planet of sorrow and pain.

The reward of these people is to see the spirit of unity gaining ground, day after day, in spite of the loud voice of separative interests.

A person of unity is not a dreamer, preacher, or visionary. He is a practical person and whatever he does he means. He gives his energy, his money, and even his life to promote unity.

His activities are based not on feelings, but sound reasoning, logic, and insight. He is an educated person. He knows clearly the motives and the techniques by which the separative spirit works. He knows how they appeal to the senses to bribe people or to force them into their camp. But in spite of the darkness that he sees in the hearts of those people who foster the spirit of separation, he never hates them. On the contrary, he cares for them and even cries for them.

It is very difficult to continue on this path of unity for a long time. Many people attempt it, but when they see the thickness of the walls of separation they feel discouraged.

But unity is the greatest challenge, and if achieved it will be the greatest reward for humanity. The spirit of unity will open for us the gates to the treasures of cosmos.

4. The fourth dimension of love is the *ability to cooperate with the Plan of the Hierarchy.*

The fire of love will purify man to such a degree that he is able to see the Plan and work for it, in cooperation with all of the heroes of the world. Greater love begins to manifest between those people who can clearly see the Plan and dedicate all their lives for the Plan.

This is a love that cannot be enjoyed in former dimensions. This is a new love which streams out from the heart of Christ and unites the lovers to such a degree that they are ready now to risk their whole life, all that they are and all that they have for the fulfillment of the Plan.

The manifestation of the Plan is the manifestation of the Soul on the individual level. It is the process in which man becomes a living Soul. As the Plan manifests through the labor of dedicated people, they are transformed into living Souls. Man can penetrate into the real mysteries of love only after he becomes a living Soul, a new born man, laboring for the Plan. You can see such a love among the disciples of Christ, and among those who are really dedicated to the upliftment of humanity.

Greater love manifests in greater challenge. Greater love manifests when a group of people face a greater responsibility for humanity. Such dedicated people may work in different fields in different nations, or religions, but all their activities are directed to unify and uplift humanity through the manifestation of the Divine Plan.

A small boy began to take violin lessons. He did well and played for many gatherings. Eventually he entered into an orchestra and played numerous symphonies. When he was asked how he felt about being in the orchestra, he answered, "All the music that I was playing was somewhat like gathering the materials to build a great cathedral. In the orchestra I saw the cathedral built and all of the musicians as inseparable parts of that cathedral, dedicated to the great architect."

What is the Plan? The Plan is the blueprint of the perfected cathedral of human spiritual and physical achievements. There will be no cathedral if the parts of the cathedral do not lose their identity in the whole construction.

People on this fourth dimension live in the Plan, for the Plan, and the Plan manifests itself through their life. Let us remember that the Plan is formed by the intuitional substance. And intuition is greater electricity of love which penetrates into the deepest layers of the human being and releases unexpected heroism and beauty from their Innermost Being.

The co-workers of the Plan are continuously influencing energy which, age after age, creates beauty within the hearts of human beings. Beauty is manifestation of the Plan.

To stand on such an elevated level of love is a difficult and dangerous task. People will tell you, "Hate."

You will say, "There is no hate in the Plan. I can't hate."

They will tell you, "Kill."

You will answer, "Just a minute. Let me see. There is no killing in the Plan."

They will say, "Separate."

You will answer, "No structure can be raised except by unity." And they will hate you because they will see you as a danger to their interests.

How shocking it is that people sell their heritage for a cup of soup![4]

People who are living on the fourth dimension of love do not react to hate. Hatred by other people releases in them new fields of enthusiasm for human betterment.

Such a love is the most purifying energy for the human body, emotions, and thoughts. It transforms the whole man.

5. The fifth dimension of love can be formulated as a *life lived for the manifestation and fulfillment of the Will or Purpose of the Great Architect*.

What is purpose? It is very easy to understand it. We have a structure built in perfect beauty. But for what purpose is it going to be used? It is possible that the builders knew only about the plan, and the workers knew only about their labor, but they never knew about the purpose of the building. On the fifth dimension of love you are able to penetrate into the purpose for which the building was erected.

As love increases, you penetrate more into the mysteries of the Creation.

The Plan states that humanity must reach relative perfection, and this planet must turn into a sacred planet. But why? What is the Purpose behind it? Is it because this planet is going to play a role in the evolution of the solar system, in the evolution of the galaxy . . . ?

The fifth dimensional love will reveal the whole mystery behind the veil. Such a mystery cannot be reflected on the mirror of our intellect if that mirror is dusty with any kind of expression against the Law of Love. A person of fifth dimensional love is a co-worker of the Purpose of the Architect.

6. The sixth dimensional *love is beyond, it is a life lived in the labor of the solar system*. Such a person takes part in the greater conscious labor going on for the perfection of the solar system.

Such people transcended the stage of humanity, and they work in the Father's Home, symbolically understood. The bond of love that exists between such people cannot be broken by any visible or invisible power.

7. The seventh dimension of love may be called a *striving toward the call of the galaxy*.

We are told that there are a few who penetrated into such a task, and they form the link between our solar system and the galaxy. They supply cosmic Love to our solar system which is distributed by those who work on lower dimensions, until it partially reaches humanity on this planet. You find a few remarks about such achievements in the *Bhagavad Gita, Vishnu Purana,* and in the *New Testament*.

Such a great love transforms the human soul into a Ray through which the creative energy of the universe is transmitted. Such great Souls are streams of blessings and bliss, and in critical times of the history of humanity they extend their help and energy to overcome crises and pave the way for the future.

People speak about space and infinity. Neither space nor Infinity can be crossed by the power of the intellect, but it can be crossed by the Power of Love. Love itself is Infinity. As your love increases, you turn into Infinity.

Those who are on the seventh dimension of love are embodiments of the Cosmic Love Ray. Only such a love bridges the Infinity, and those who can come in contact with such streams of Divine Love can see the new vision of cosmic synthesis.

The level of our love attracts those conditions in which we live. We see that the royal road of victory is the road of love. Only on such a path, step by step, do we synchronize ourselves with the Cosmic Magnet which is drawing each human Spark toward beauty, unity, cooperation, identification, and into total synthesis. This is the path of *becoming oneself*. Stage after stage man finds his true Self, until he reaches the stage on which he finds and becomes one with his Cosmic Self.

Christ once said, "Whoever wants to find himself must lose himself."

The process of losing oneself is accomplished in ever increasing love. It is a process of losing the false self and finding the real Self, the real Self within him, within all men, and within all creation.

How can we progress on the path of love? The answer will be—

increase your love, engage yourself in loving activities, and express love through your emotions and feelings. Think through love. Love your neighbor as you love yourself. Every day do something that is based on your loving understanding. Every time you feel that you did something against the spirit of love, correct it, and see why you did it, and try not to repeat it.

There is also another way to increase your love energy. Once a week think about those who suffer because of injustice, exploitation and hatred, and see what you need to develop within you to help those people. Many great organizations came into being in response to human suffering. Love must be manifested in practical actions. It is practical action that changes love into love-wisdom.

Wisdom uses love in accordance with need, and in harmony with the Plan. In our Four Freedoms, we have

Freedom of speech
Freedom of worship
Freedom from want
Freedom from fear

We lack all these freedoms because of lack of love. Once we love, our speech is free. We are free to worship. All our needs are met, and our fear is gone. So we can add another line under the Four Freedoms and say that

Freedom of speech
Freedom of worship
Freedom from want
Freedom from fear

can be sustained only by love.

All our problems in these four fields of freedom are the result of lack of love.

A true love thinks first of others, and this thinking develops in such a way that a man eventually cares for all beings.

Love affects our vehicles and attitudes.

In the first dimension, giving changes the inertia of our physical life into activity, and even into rhythm. This is because giving demands action, organization, discrimination, labor. A giving man tires of accumulating and gives more. This demands skill in action, discipline of time and matter and education. All of these eventually put the physical mechanism in the highest order.

On the second dimension, when a man tries to stand for beauty, he cleanses his glamors. Beauty puts a heavy demand on his nature to respond to Divine Harmony within his true Self. Glamor is a distortion of love. As true love increases, the distortion vanishes.

On the third dimension—love for unity—we see the dispersing of illusions. Illusions are based on the spirit of separatism. Unity establishes rhythm, not only on the mental plane, but also on the emotional and physical planes.

We may say also that all the disorders and illnesses of the personality are the result of inertia, glamor, and illusion.

These three dimensions of love eventually heal the personality and make it a vital mechanism for great service.

The disappearance of maya, glamor, and illusion sets the flow of psychic energy free, which circulates in the mechanism of personality and directs its activities in harmony with the Cosmic Symphony.

Love energy becomes more effective and inclusive as it is expressed through higher and higher planes. Physical, emotional, and mental love is all that the majority of people come into contact with.

The Source of greater love is found in our Solar Angel. This is a term which refers to the transpersonal Self, higher Self, or the Inner Guide.

Another great Source of love is the Spiritual Triad. The Spiritual Triad is the combined sphere of love, light, and power within the higher planes of man. It channels fiery love from the corresponding Center of the planet.

Christ, Who is the embodiment of Cosmic Love, said once, "Be courageous, I have overcome the world."

Chapter 6

THE WISDOM OF LOVE

"Verily, when one learns to inculcate the emanations of feeling, one will see that precisely love above all attracts the fire of space. He who said, 'Love one another,' was a true Yogi . . ."[1]

NE DAY I WAS SITTING on a beautiful green hill, deeply engaged in study, when a young couple approached me. They were troubled and began to speak to me of their problem. I learned that they were planning to marry, but that the girl had suffered a nervous breakdown and had been hospitalized for three weeks. She had been released only that day, and the young man was anxious that I see her and talk to her. I gently asked her, "What is the matter? What is troubling you?"

Without hesitation she replied, "I went to the Father confessor and he told me that I will burn in hell because I have loved this man. When I went to my mother, she said, 'I have nothing but disgust for you. I hate you.' Then I turned to my father and he shouted, 'You must leave this house at once!' Now, I don't know what to do. I just hate everybody!"

"Do you know," I said, "you can be happy?"

133

"How," she cried, "how can I be happy?"

"It is very simple," I answered, "just start loving."

"But whom can I love?" she asked, "Whom can I trust and love?"

"Listen carefully," I said, "and I will tell you about a little drama we are going to have right here on this beautiful hill. First, you are going to run to that pine tree. You are going to hold that pine tree with both arms, kiss it and tell it that you love it. Next, you will go to that lovely rose and tell it the same thing. After that, you will lie down on the grass and love the grass. When you have done all these things, you will come back to me and I will tell you something."

She paused for a moment and said, "I will do as you say." She ran to the pine tree and threw her arms around it. I felt that she was crying because of the length of time she clung to the great trunk of the tall pine.

"Come," I encouraged her, "the next one."

With tears in her eyes she knelt before the rose, the little rose just opening. Holding the blossom tenderly with both hands, I heard her say, "You know I love you. Do you love me?"

She arose and started to cry as she took a few steps forward and flung herself upon the soft green grass. Lying there quietly, she uttered these simple words, "I love you, grass."

I called to her, "Come here and look at the setting sun. Just cry out to the sun and ask, 'Sun, do you love me? I love you because you are the light!'"

The rich quality of her voice was unbelievable. It was joy, ecstasy, freedom. It revealed a striving to break something, to jump forth into reality. After a few moments she sat down, quietly, peacefully, and said,

"I love nature. I love everything. I love my mother no matter what she says or does. I love my father and my priest, but I know that I am not going to burn."

"No, if everything loves you, how can you burn?"

This is one of the mysteries of love. I was certain that it would not be necessary for her to be hospitalized again. As they were leaving, she pushed her friend away, saying, "I am going to drive."

The young man was perplexed. This young woman had changed so much in the matter of a few minutes that he was at a loss to

understand it. He did not know what to do about letting her drive the car. I said, "Let her drive."
"Will it be safe? Do you have faith in her?" he asked.
"Of course I have," I replied.
Then I said to the girl, "Before you go, kiss me."
When she kissed me I said to her, "I, also love you."
"You do?" she said, smiling.
"Yes, of course," I replied. "From now on everything will love you—the trees, the birds, the flowers, everybody."
The love energy had been released in her. When you suppress, within your heart, the greatest energy in the universe, you burn with that energy, you are cracked with that energy; but if you release it, you are sane and harmonious. You are a rhythmic note in the Symphony of the Universe. Thus you grow and bloom with the universe, with the cosmos.
Love is communication, communion, and responsiveness. All growth, enlightenment, evolution, and progress depend on "the unfolding of a continually increasing power to respond." Life is communication, communion. We are not speaking of the ordinary life which we live, but of Life-energy, which makes us breathe, think, and grow. This is communion, itself. It is Love.
Life is oneness. Unless it is one, there is no life. Oneness means livingness, communion. Separation, division leads to death. Closer relationship means deeper life; less relationship means less life. All parts are related to the whole.
We can start with man and say, a finger cannot live without becoming a part of the hand; the hand cannot live without the body; the body cannot live without communication with the world as a whole, a chemical world, air and sun. Earth cannot support life if it has no communication with the sun. Such relationships are outer communication, or responses.
Responses of a mechanism to a greater mechanism create livingness, but this livingness reaches higher and higher dimensions when you start with conscious responses. Mechanical life will lead you to a certain level, but to continue upward from there to higher levels, you will need to unfold other levels of response—emotional response and mental response. Our livingness depends upon the radius of our emotional response, and upon the width and depth of our mental response.

Emotional response is a process of detecting the emotional needs of a person and fulfilling his needs on the emotional level. Mental response is the process of knowing a person as he stands in his mental activities, and meeting his needs on the mental level. When your ability to respond lifts itself to the higher mental or causal plane, you come into direct realization of the person involved; you see him in the light of the greater whole, greater unity, and your love increases and becomes purer.

In the next step, we enter into the world of pure love. In esoteric teaching this world is known as the world of Intuition, or the sphere of straight knowledge. It is here that our love breaks all of its limitations and embraces the *whole*.

Life is communication, an act of loving response and harmonization, a tuning in with higher and higher levels of awareness and beingness.

All wars, all pain, all troubles are due to crystallization. Sometimes, somewhere the flow of energy stops, becomes crystallized and no longer circulates freely. When crystallization occurs, you have religious, political, and social upheavals bringing great suffering to many. Break the crystallizations, permitting greater responses and you will have more life, more joy, and more happiness.

Religious and political prejudice and intolerance are crystallizations, a "drying-up," in the channel of energy circulation. Hatred and jealousy are emotional level crystallizations which block circulation of energy. Ignorance and illusion are mental level crystallizations. Break through these crystallizations and you have more life. Try to communicate with your Soul and Spirit; communicate with the best in the physical, emotional, and mental worlds. Find the Inner Center of conscious energy. Find your goal in life. Real communication starts when *you are yourself*.

The steps toward reaching that Inner Core are:
Discipline
Concentration
Meditation
Contemplation
Livingness
Only through such steps can you meet yourself and respond to real love energy. This love cannot be learned, responded to or communicated through philosophy, psychology, or by listening

to lectures—but through loving. The one way to learn the meaning of love is to love. Once you have loved, then and only then, can you know love. It takes you away. It sublimates you, releases you, and instead of becoming a self-centered man or woman, you become Universe-centered, Cosmos-centered; thus is love energy released.

In our modern world, when people speak of "Love," they usually understand it to be largely concerned with sex. They are not wrong providing they are truly aware of what sex really is. Sex is communication between energy and matter, between Spirit and substance; communication to carry on the Purpose of the Cosmic Being, to give expression to that Cosmic Aim or Purpose for which by which and through which, this whole cosmos is created. All of creation is the result of sex; energy and matter coming together. In a religious or philosophical sense, it is said, when Spirit and matter come together, they create all of the universes. Love is all-embracing energy. All atoms, all cells are imbued with it. Actually, it is this love energy which is making greater and greater mechanisms through which to express itself in greater beauty.

The mineral, vegetable, and animal kingdoms are vehicles of expression for love energy. We may even say that one of the original long-range goals of this love energy was to create man, who eventually will express love consciously, and then be a co-worker with the Creative Energy.

What is the origin of this Energy? In one occult book, there is a very interesting and picturesque expression of the Energy Source. It states that there are three Suns which give light to the whole universe. Behind the visible sun, is the Heart of the Sun, which is the Source of the Love—the outpouring Love of the Creator. Hidden behind that Sun is the Central Spiritual Sun, which is the Source of Life. It is the second Sun with which we are concerned, for it is the Source of Love. It is all-embracing compassion, and in esoteric literature is called the Great Magnet, or the Great Mother, which continually attracts all Sparks back to Herself. Through this attraction process which we call love, each Spark in the mineral, vegetable, animal, or human kingdoms—no matter how deeply encased in matter they become—is attracted to that Central Core, the Cosmic Magnet, which is inhaling it slowly, drawing it back to Its Home. This is evolution.

If we review the history of humanity we see that a man becomes a family; a family becomes a group; a group becomes a nation; and nations become united nations. We know, that no matter what happens, that Great Magnet will pave the way for one humanity as it attracts the individuals, blending them into greater units, greater wholes. Through greater communication, responses, greater harmony and cooperation among the Sparks, among the living souls, all of creation will slowly become a Whole Symphony, unfolding the Mystery of Love.

There is only one great science and that science is the Science of Love. Love is nothing but Electrical Energy. If a man has hatred radiations or if a man has jealousy, his vibrations are different, his aura is different and the color of the atmosphere around him is different. If, however, that man is full of Love Energy, he is radioactive, free; whatever he touches blooms, is released, has gained its freedom.

We must know how to use this energy as a good electrician knows the laws of electricity, and uses them. He very carefully observes and obeys the laws because he is aware of the fact that in working with electricity, he can lose his life or bring light and many other blessings to us. How can we deal with this Science of Love so that the Love Energy really fulfills the Purpose behind it? If a man loves without knowledge of the Laws of Energy, he can burn himself. Most of our sufferings, our agonies, our pain, our breakdowns, are caused by so-called "love." We may hear such words as, "Oh, that girl rejected me!" "My wife divorced me!" "My son isn't interested in me!" It is all love matter.

All human relationships are based on this great Energy, Love, and yet we must educate ourselves to use it as an electrician must be trained prior to attempting to work with electrical energy.

True love is life. In loving, you have more life and you give more life because you are tuning in with Cosmic Love, which is the substance of unity, cooperation, understanding, synthesis, harmony, and beauty.

THE PATH OF LOVE

There are eight steps on the path of love:

1. LOVE MUST BE PROGRESSIVELY EXPANDING

This means that your love must not stop at sex, but must climb upward toward greater unity, progressing toward higher levels of existence, and revealing itself in higher forms of creativity and service.

The downfall of families, of great men and women, of groups and organizations—ancient and modern—is the result of a love that was largely concentrated on the sex level; a love that was not progressively moving from the physical level toward higher levels— emotional, mental, and spiritual levels.

The purpose of Love Energy is to express Divinity Itself, on all levels. This is what creativity is. In every act of love, on any level, this uplifting Cosmic Purpose must be realized.

You must always know whether your love limits itself or progresses toward freedom. A loving person must be able to say, "I love myself, but I love you also. I love you as a group of people; but not just all of you, I love your whole nation. I love not only your nation, I love all nations, I love all humanity. My love does not stop there, I love our solar system. I stand on the mountain and behold the beauty of the stars, and I say, 'I love you.'"

If love stops somewhere and you say, "I love, but I love myself— not you," it is a poison. The electrical system has a short circuit somewhere. Because of this one little short circuit, all of your light is gone. By using Love Energy in this way, people become dark, poisonous, hateful, jealous, separative. Love must be expanding, expanding, ever expanding. . . . Thus, not only must you love the visible universe, you must also love the invisible universe, Divine Energies, Divine Ideas, Great Concepts. For example, people say, "This is the only way to fly!" This is not true. You are dividing and belittling yourself, narrowing and squeezing yourself. Just be open as a little child is open and embrace the cosmos. If your love is progressive, you are becoming a co-worker of the Great Cosmic Heart, the Great Magnet.

When your love is not progressive, and when your love cannot create something higher than sexual satisfaction, you become weaker and you experience a feeling of dissatisfaction, failure, loneliness, all of which lead you toward carelessness, inertia, and death.

True love must start from higher levels, perhaps from spiritual levels, and pass downward to perform creative, therapeutic and releasing work to create unity on the three lower levels, and then climb back to the Source from whence it originated.

If a little chicken says, "I want to stay in my shell, I do not want to grow bigger," that little chicken dies; his life is snuffed out. But if that chicken breaks its shell and says, "I want to crack, to destroy my limitations (those limitations against love, any hindrances to love), I want to crack my shell and get out," then you have a beautiful chicken. It opens its eyes and wonders at the beautiful outside world. If you were a chicken, imagine what you would feel if you suddenly came out of the shell. "My! This is my mother; this is my father. What are these beautiful things—flowers?" Feel the joy! That joy is expansion; joy of freedom; joy of greater harmony, relationship, and communication.

Love starts from lower levels also. Let us say I love a girl, but I love only her body; beyond that I cannot pass, so my love will crystallize. That love will be very short. I try to expand that love toward her heart, then toward her mind, but if I stop there, again the love will stagnate. I must pass beyond the mental and enter into the spiritual levels; and if, in so doing, I can raise that girl and myself together, my love is finding consummation, love is expanding and becoming creative. If at any moment love stops expanding, you can expect trouble from your physical, emotional, and mental bodies. That is the Science of Love.

If you say, for example, "I love my nation, but I hate that other nation," this hatred may eventually create such tension that fifty or sixty thousand, or a million people, could be sacrificed in war. But love bridges all. Love cultivates understanding and cooperation.

Marriage or love is not only the unity of two bodies. We marry with our hearts if we are dedicated to the same goal. We can marry with our ideas, our thoughts, our visions, and receive greater satisfaction than from a marriage based on the physical level. Those who have physical intercourse and do not have intercourse between their higher natures, feel empty and neglected after the lower physical nature has been satisfied. If, however, intercourse is on higher levels as well as the physical level, the result is joy and expansion of consciousness.

There is a story in the Far East that tells of a king who had in his household many beautiful young girls who swam naked in a pool every day. Once each week the king would send his only son down to the pool to bring up a bucket of water. Always however, when the young man went down to the pool, he was so charmed by the girls that he did not return. The king would have to go to the pool, bring him back, and send him hunting to make him forget the beautiful maidens. One day the son asked,

"Father, why did you not let me stay with them?"

"I am glad you have asked me," said the king. "Until you learn to go to the pool and obey the order by returning promptly; until you can go and return without being swayed by their charms, you will not be allowed to remain with them."

This simple story portrays the principle of self-control, the principal of sublimation, economy, and the meaning of purposeful love. Let us remember that the purpose of love is to take us back to Divine Unity, into the Cosmic Magnet. This being the case, each act of love must be a step toward Home.

2. THE NATURE OF LOVE IS SACRIFICIAL

There is no love without sacrifice. Love is giving—not taking. There is no expectation in love. Love must be sacrificial. If I say, "I love you," and stand behind my love, if I sacrifice for you, then my love is supported and I am proving that it is a real love.

At one time I was speaking in a private college. As part of the program, another man gave an excellent talk in which he said that we must build fine colleges because they are divine temples. His speech was beautiful and well delivered. When he came and sat by me, I said,

"Write a check."

"What?" he asked.

"Write a check so that we can build that college. You have the money."

"Later," he replied.

"Then," I admonished him, "you are not standing behind your love."

When you say "love," you must sacrifice. If you do not sacrifice, you are not a lover, no matter what! You may ask, "Sacrifice what?" There is no end to it. In sacrifice, you are giving up your egoism, your separation, your materialism, your self-centeredness; you are sacrificing all that is dear to you for the upliftment of another being who is part of yourself. That is what love is. You are, one by one, breaking the bars by which you are imprisoned. You are destroying the crystallized materialism within yourself. You are breaking up the crystallized concept that you are a separated being. Once you have given of yourself, you have proved that you are loving.

Recently a husband said to me, "My wife loves me very much, but when I ask her to make a certain dish, or to prepare a little more food to eat, she says, 'Honey, let's go to a restaurant.' "

Later I met his wife and I said, "You are such a pretty girl. Do you love your husband?"

She answered, "Yes, of course."

"All right," I said, "make some sacrifice for him. Start with the A-B-C's. Prepare some special dish which he likes. Do little things for him, so that eventually you will learn to sacrifice more, for greater purposes, greater aims, greater destinations, and without expectation."

Every time you "love" without sacrifice, you create a complex situation in your inner world. You create congestion. This can be avoided if you will stand behind your love and express it through your *practical* sacrifices. If you love and do not express your love with sacrifice, the fire of love burns your mental, emotional, and etheric centers creating in them insensitivity, dullness, ulcers, and many other unwholesome conditions. Every time you love and are not making sacrifices for it you are touching electrical energy which may burn you. It is said that our God is burning fire.

If you say to a beloved one, "I love you," but refrain from performing sacrificial acts to meet that person's various needs, your love is selfish. If you fail to make sacrifices necessary to uplift and to reach a deeper stage of understanding and creativity, your love is selfish. Selfishness is a state of mind in which the channel of love is congested. The Love Energy cannot circulate and communicate with the greater whole. Selfishness stops the transmutation of matter. Love causes transmutation of matter. The matter of your vehicles must be transmuted into higher sensitivity, enabling you to create under higher spiritual impulses.

The goal of a human being, of a nation, of humanity, is not

survival. Survival is a station on the eternal path of spiritualization. The ultimate goal of any living being is to express beauty, and to be beautiful. There is a great Symphony in the Mind of Cosmos. Each act performed to increase our capacity to "feel," to be "impressed" by the Symphony, and each effort to express it in our individual and global life, is an act of touching the beauty, a step toward the realization of beauty. This is accomplished only through the acts of creative loving.

The true Love Energy emanates from the Heart of the Sun. This energy cannot be contacted until a man actually enters into the Intuitional level of awareness through real acts of sacrifice. Oddly enough, mothers, because of their nature, have access to this energy in their dedication and sacrifice. When dedication and sacrifice are withdrawn, they lose the true contact with love. Once love is lost, ugliness starts. No man or woman is handsome, pretty or beautiful without love.

3. LOVE IS THE MIDWIFE OF BEAUTY

There are three active energies—light, love, and power; or life. The life and love and light of our three bodies are given by the visible sun; it is the source of our light, electricity, love, and life on three levels. On the fourth level, the Intuitional, the Heart of the Sun becomes active for us, and a higher love starts to penetrate into the heart of the human being. On special occasions, a certain extra quantity of such love is given to the individual. For example, a woman receives her higher love energy at the time of conception, and an additional amount at the time of delivery. The father receives higher energy at the time of the first intercourse with the mother, providing the act is sacred, conscious and accepted. The child receives it through breast-feeding and the love of his mother. At puberty, another quota of higher love is given to both sexes.

The amount of love is occasionally increased through acts of sacrifice or conscious suffering, but a human being truly starts to love when he comes into conscious contact with the reservoir of love on the Intuitional level. The brotherhood of humanity will be possible when the majority of men contact the Intuitional level. For this reason we are urged to expand our consciousness, because in expanding our consciousness, we will become more brotherly and closer to the concept of the brotherhood of man.

When light and life energy are used without love, the trend is toward materialism, possession, separation, all of which are forms of hatred.

Love energy given to animals, to trees, to insects, at certain times, is used largely in procreation, or in cooperation with nature. It is like a heartbeat which is distributing love energy in cycles to lower kingdoms, and to the human kingdom.

Because the greater portion of humanity is oriented physically, emotionally, and mentally, love energy is translated through the contents of these levels, and used for satisfaction on these three levels only. This indicates that man can increase his quota of love energy by the performance of special acts and through self exertion. The greatest way to increase love energy is through the labor of responsibility which results in sacrificial acts.

4. THE UNCONDITIONAL NATURE OF LOVE

The unconditional nature of love stands behind these beautiful words spoken by Christ, "Greater love hath no man than this, that a man lay down his life for his friends." You love, not because you are expecting hundreds of dollars, great fame and glory, or a great reputation, but because the fulfillment of the Purpose of the Cosmos is that you, as a drop, give yourself and love more. People say, "If you love me, I will love you." This is not love. Can you love a man who hates you? Can you love a man who has blackened your name, slandered your reputation? Can you still say, "I love you and I am going to stand by you and help you in any way you may need my help." This is *unconditional* love.

As you become love, you become stronger, more magnetic, more understanding, more powerful and influential; and slowly, very slowly, others will see that you are a rich, radiating beauty. You inspire them; you take them from the low state in which they are living; you crack their self-centeredness. If you save only one man, only one woman, you have done the greatest work in the cosmos because, as is said in the scriptures, great joys are witnessed and recorded in heaven if a man turns toward the light, toward love. All over the world we are short on love; hence the many kinds of sorrow, pain, suffering, debts, and crimes.

When love, pouring down from the Heart of the Sun, is assimilated and used to build a path toward the Cosmic Magnet, that distorted noise which we call the universe and humanity, will slowly change into a Great Symphony, and every man everywhere will love, will understand. When this glorious change comes to pass, this planet, instead of being a planet of sorrow, a planet of pain and suffering, will be a planet of joy, freedom, and liberation. Those who are moving toward greater blooming are sensing the greatest joy, even though their physical, emotional, and mental natures are passing through strain or stress. They have great joy because they are communicating with the Source of Divine Joy, the Great Cosmic Love.

In real love, the lover is lost in the loved one. He or she exists for the loved one. Thus is unity performed. Such love is not an emotional outpouring, but the result of an intuitional urge in which one feels that whatever he is doing is absolutely the right thing to do. It is not a blind emotional drive, or a desire, but clear reason and identification with the lover.

When our love increases in spite of conditions, we become able to touch the life-saving energy. If it decreases because of existing conditions, we have not yet tasted the joy of real love, which is all-giving, under all conditions.

5. RESPONSIBILITY IS ONE OF THE LAWS OF THE SCIENCE OF LOVE

Love performed without a sense of responsibility, leads us to sorrow and suffering. Responsibility means that you will sustain unity once you have created it, and work for the progressive advancement of that unity toward more love, more light, and more life. Responsibility teaches you that other people's failures and sorrows are yours, and that you must try to eliminate them physically, emotionally, and mentally with freedom and joy, as if they were yours.

Ask yourself, "Am I ready to face my responsibilities?" If you can face them you are really loving, but if you are escaping you are degenerating. It is a very difficult thing because love is our life. Wherever we go, we meet it. It is everywhere. If you make a selfish move, you will suffer; you will cause suffering. It was because of this that in olden times, one of the ancient races used to teach the subject of love to people before they entered into marriage. What a beautiful idea; that man must know what love is— spiritual love, unity, beauty, understanding, cooperation, harmony, great sacrifice—before he is able to lift someone up to that level in his marriage or love.

6. THE NON-SEPARATIVE NATURE OF LOVE—MAN IS NOT REALLY LOVING IF HE DOES NOT LOVE EVERYTHING IN CREATION

Is this surprising? Everything must be loved, even your ugliness or your beauty. Nothing must be left out—trees, birds, fish, sky—everything in the universe must be loved until you feel that YOU ARE LOVE ITSELF. This is very important, because many people think that they love if they say, "I love you, dear," or a person may say, "I love you so much, but I hate your neighbor." Here you are short of love. Love must be a unified, cosmic, all embracing love.

I know a medical doctor who wrote a beautiful article about love. After reading it I said to him,

"Doctor, you really know the biology of love, and I assume that you really do love, too?"

"Of course," he said. "I love my wife."

"I didn't mean that." I said, "Is your love really as all-embracing, all-forgiving as the sun?"

"Hum," he said. "I guess so."

Later, on a very stormy night, at two o'clock in the morning, he called me.

"Oh. Come quick! I have killed my wife!"

"You are crazy!" I said.

I hurried to his home. It was true. He had shot his wife, because he had found her talking to another man. Now this man may know the biology of love, but he does not know what love is.

If you read the newspapers all over the world, you can see and feel and intuitively understand what jealousy does; what a miserable unhappy life it brings to wives, children, husbands, and friends. I do not think the world can be changed by armies. It has never been done that way, but the world can be changed by love alone. No matter what we do, or do not do, the Love Energy pulls us toward unity, through suffering.

One hundred years ago we were very separated in the world. But what do we have now? We have the United States, United Kingdom, United Republics, and now, United Nations. Then why not think that the next step will be United Humanity? All these unities are the result of the human response to that outpouring Solar Love.

You cannot have real love in your heart if you love one person and hate another person, another race, another religion, another nation, another culture; because love is the Current of Energy taking you toward unity, toward the Great Synthesis.

7. JOY IS A CHARACTERISTIC OF LOVE

Anytime you think about or sense love, you think about joy. There is no love if there is no joy. Any sacrifice, any act of love, will be an act of joy; because physically, emotionally, mentally, and spiritually when you are loving you are in great joy. You are radiating joy, because joy and love are the same energy. If at any time you see that in your love there is no joy, then there is something wrong. You must adjust yourself, adjust the conditions and try to find the focus; when you have found the focus, you have found the joy.

In one of His greatest, most critical moments, Jesus, looking at the people who were crucifying Him, said, "My Lord, forgive them, for they know not what they do." Imagine this outpouring love! What great love this is—that in the last moment, when there is almost no blood left in His veins, He is saying, ". . . forgive them."

8. GRATITUDE

Gratitude is so beautiful. Are you grateful? If in your love there is no gratefulness, there is no love. This is one of the greatest problems in our lives, in our social, family, and international life. Gratitude is the appreciation, the recognition of love. Let us be grateful to trees, to flowers, to birds, to sunshine, to the rivers, to the oceans, to all men, known or unknown, who have helped us, who have created our culture. Let us be grateful for our suffering, for our harsh lessons, for existence as a whole, because all is love, essentially, and all must become love again. If we are blind to the offerings of nature, to the hands that have helped us, to the conditions that have made us grow and unfold, we close ourselves to the life-giving current of love, and invite pain and suffering.

Gratitude is a higher form of communication. It is a way to radiate our blessings. It is a way of showing appreciation for the

Fountainhead of all joy, of all love. A grateful man becomes healthier, more magnetic, more enduring, more patient, and all of his acts become creative. Only in gratitude is the Love Energy of Cosmos assimilated and changed into creative and uplifting energy.

Gratitude is a state of being in which man communicates with the energy of the will-to-good, with the energy of right human relations. It is a state of being which enables man to see the working of karma, and to trust himself to the arms of the Divine Love.

All those who are striving for the common good, for the upliftment of humanity, eventually will be drawn together by the Energy of Love, will be galvanized by the Power of Love, and will act according to the Law of Unity, through cooperation and understanding. Thus will be created a new culture, a new civilization in which man will live in sacrificial service for all humanity.

True love will be recognized as a process of diminishing the flame of our separating selves, and increasing the fire of the Great Whole within ourselves. This is the way to clear our path for the glorious Future.

All our past debts, which have accumulated because of our wrong deeds, emotional reactions, and mental activities can be paid in a life of more loving. This means that love leads us into more freedom on the path of return. This means that loving increases our joy, our bliss, our understanding, and our health on all levels. To love, means to tune into our Self, the greatest creative power "from Whom all things proceed and to Whom all things return." Thus a man becomes a Creator and a Fountain of Life.

". . . We welcome each transport of love and self-sacrifice. As a lever sets the wheels in motion, so love sets up the strongest reaction. Compared with the radiance of love, the strongest hatred reflects only as a hideous mark. For love is the true reality and treasure."[2]

"The word that issues from the heart saturates the space."[3]

Chapter 7

LOVE

RUE LOVE IS THE magnetic energy radiating from the Divine Spark in man.

Man essentially is a drop of the Supreme Energy, which we call "love."

Most of the people we see around us are not men; they are machines, or plants, or at best they are bodies. The *real* man is a Christ, a person who is able to experience his own Essential Divinity.

To give a graphic explanation, we can draw the following diagram:

149

LIFE

| DIVINE 7 | | ∞ | | DIVINE UNLIMITED |

MONADIC 6		10,000		ONENESS
SPIRITUAL 5		900		RHYTHM
INTUITIONAL 4		700		HARMONY
MENTAL 3		500		GOODWILL
EMOTIONAL 2		200		RIGHT HUMAN RELATIONS
PHYSICAL ATTRACTION 1		25		SEX
CHEMICAL AFFINITY		2		MOLECULAR ATTRACTION

DEATH

From the above graph, we see that love extends and unfolds as it ascends. The lowest point is called death. The highest point is life; life increases proportionally to love. When love increases, life increases.

Every union is fulfilled by love energy. If two bodies are coming together, it is love that brings them together, but it is a love working through the physical body. If the love deepens, it means that the higher level, emotional plane love, has started to express itself. In this case the two persons come closer to each other.

If love starts to express itself through the mental plane of both parties, the energy of attraction gets stronger. These two individuals practically register one another's feeling and thinking. They start to live in right relations, and goodwill dominates their thoughts and activities.

When these individuals pass into the intuitional consciousness, or awareness, they start to sense the real taste of love. They feel the Love-energy in the universe. They sense it in green pastures, in the music of trees, in the flowers and mountains, in the birds and animals, in the stars and the waves of the sea, for they live in the ocean of love. Love makes them bloom.

I read once about a man who bought some wheat from the market and took it to his village. Upon his arrival at the village, he noticed that there were many ants in the wheat. He was very distressed for he thought the poor ants would have a very difficult time away from their own home, so he walked five miles and took them back to the bazaar where he had purchased the wheat.

This is a sense of love which is extended toward little creatures, because this man was able to feel unity with ants also.

Another story which impressed me very much is this: A young and beautiful village girl got up early in the morning and went to the well to draw some water with a bucket that was hinged by a rope. Suddenly she noticed that a climbing vine had entwined itself around the rope and flourished there with a lovely blue flower. She thought that if she let the bucket run down into the well, the flower's tender stem would be cut and the lovely flower's life would be destroyed. So she proceeded to her neighbor and asked, "My dear neighbor would you please give me a bucket of water to wash my face? A little flower is holding the rope of our well and I don't want to cut it."

On the Spiritual level, love expresses itself as revelation. Through unity and identification man becomes aware of the hearts and thoughts of people. He reads their hearts and minds and nothing is hidden from his eyes. Meanwhile, he radiates a healing energy through his thoughts, emotions, and activities. His eyes and words heal, uplift, and lead you into the freedom of life. Under his influence a transmutation process starts in your life.

At the Divine level, man touches the Essential Electrical and Magnetic Love. He becomes a transmitter of all healing, bridging, purifying, and enlightening energies. He becomes a co-worker of the Divine Plan.

This is the path of love, which starts from the chemical affinity and takes you into the ocean of unity. This is the path of glory, of victory, of achievement, of Divinity. It starts from the zero point and ascends to Infinity. The more you love, the more you are; the more you love, the more life you have—and the more glory, more perfection, more achievement, more joy, and more bliss you have.

The value of man is determined by where he stands on the ladder of love. He is a man of second degree value if he is living on the second step of the ladder. His value is 200, if he is living on step

200. You can ascend the ladder of love toward Infinity, for the life of immortality passes only through the ladder of love. Once you reach universal love, you receive universal joy, even through a pure kiss, through a love smile, through a handshake, through a touch, through a word.

Your ascent up the love ladder does not limit your joy on lower levels. On the contrary, after you have advanced to higher levels of love, any love action on lower levels brings in the bliss of the higher planes and leads you into ecstasy. This is how some very advanced saints speak with God: through the smile of a baby, through the song of a nightingale, through the beauty of a flower, or they touch God when they touch their beloved one.

Love is happiness on physical, emotional, and mental planes. It is joy on the Soul level; it is bliss on the Spiritual plane. Whenever you use love, you have a sense of expansion, freedom, unfoldment, and creativity.

Every man has this magnetic substance of love within him; however, because of the lack of integration and development, man cannot express it as an active unit, as an active whole. He uses it in parts, and selectively, and thus limits the joy and the usefulness of Love-energy. Suppose your body loves another body. You enjoy it, but this enjoyment does not last if your heart does not love the heart of the other person.

You have fun for the present, but if you are not extending your love into the future too, then your love will not last, and every time you lose the object of your love you suffer, because you are limited. You are going down the scale, closer to inertia, closer to death.

Love is truly love only when it is used as a whole for Infinity. Master Morya says very beautifully,

". . . It is correctly pointed out that love is a leading and creative principle. It means that love must be conscious, striving, self-denying. Creativeness requires these conditions."[1]

Inspiration for creative works, or heroic and sacrificial actions is nothing else but a downpouring of love. As deep as man goes into the Energy of Love, proportionally he becomes more creative, and more radioactive.

To create means to bring out the harmony, the rhythm of love from higher levels, or to awaken the love principle from the hearts of men. *All beauties are materialized love!* People think that consciousness and love are separate things. Consciousness is love in action. We canot say "conscious love," because there is no conscious love. There is only limited love, and limited love is selfishness and darkness. Remember the wonderful expression in the Bible when the "beloved disciple" says,

"Those who love live in light."

Of course this refers to the complete love, to the whole, inclusive love, a love that extends on all planes of existence. Only through love do we understand; only through love do we recognize each other as well as ourselves. Because love is light, a light that reveals, unfolds and penetrates, the knowledge gained by love is true knowledge.

Love Energy cannot be developed and grow deeper until it creates response. Only through response can it turn into a creative energy. On whatever level Love Energy evokes response, on that same level it becomes creative.

A rejected or an ignored Love Energy crystallizes and produces a hindering force which spreads into the mechanism of the person and creates psychological disturbances and sickness. This condition gradually produces more difficulties between the two parties until separation and then a total indifference toward each other becomes an established fact. Or love changes into a selfish attacking force which we call hatred. Hatred is a demanding love, a love that wants to possess. If the person cannot possess, he tries to destroy the object of love so that others do not possess it. This is how love turns into rejection. Hatred never recognizes the good in the other person but only the wicked parts, and as the hating one concentrates his force upon the weaknesses of the other party, he increases the wickedness in himself, and thus bcomes a destructive force in the world of men.

That is why the leaders of the race often advise us to forget, forgive, and try to remain indifferent, because the worst attachment is the attachment of hatred. Unconsciously, we copy those things we hate; forgiveness and forgetfulness is a process through which we dissipate the accumulated, rejecting, and negative forces which are continuously poisoning our psychological and physical mechism. Through forgiveness and forgetfulness we release these crystallized forces and change them into Love Energies.

All creation is the effect of love. Man cannot create except through love. If he is using only 25 degrees of love, his creations will have a corresponding value. If he is creating from a high level, say from 900 degrees, then his creation will have a similar value. For example, if in our love action, we are tuned only to physical love, our children will be lower level human beings. If in our act of love, we are tuned to a very high level, we will draw into our sphere of life greater souls, more advanced beings. That is why in the olden days, Masters of the Wisdom gave special meditations in the *Upanishads*, which are to be performed before the act of love to attract a more advanced being into incarnation.

In mystic literature, the higher levels of consciousness and realizations are explained through the metaphor of spiritual marriage between bride and groom. This is truly so, because in real and higher love, man loses his selfhood and merges in the other and becomes one. If this unity is on higher levels, then the joy and bliss are real. You can compare this joy of higher realizations only with the bliss that you can register with expressed love. You feel that you are lost in another, you find yourself in the other, and together you become a complete being. In such instances, you lose these negative elements which prevent complete merging and when these elements are eliminated, the free flow of love makes the two— one. Then you feel that the other being is you.

However, the ecstasy does not stop there; it passes upward to the hearts, and the two hearts start to merge into each other. On this level starts the real joy of unity. Two divine musical compositions merge into each other and a symphony starts to flow through their hearts. Their hearts become greater and embrace the whole universe. At the time of the merging of the hearts, the couple feel a sense of nobility, sublime feelings of beauty, purity, kindness, forgetfulness, forgiveness, holiness, and an urge to sacrifice themselves for each other.

The current of love does not stop there; it carries them upward toward the mental plane. Here their minds merge, giving a rare sensation of joy. Out of this unity comes a unified purpose: to lead a life of radiation, service, and dedication.

The oneness of these three levels goes deeper and deeper until suddenly, the two Sparks unite within them and complete bliss is radiated throughout all their being. They are now one body, one heart, one mind, and one Spirit. The love vibrates throughout all their bodies, and cleans out all mental, emotional, and physical obstacles through its purifying currents. This is the age-long work for which we are called. Life by life, we build a few steps higher and higher, until one day the ladder of love is built and the souls can meet each other and be one.

The eternal pilgrim passes through forests and deserts; he finds and loses his mate; until one day his age-long labor finds its consummation and the two meet each other. Blessed is the moment when they meet!

People think that as soon as they marry, they will have complete happiness. This is a wishful expectation which often ends in sorrow and suffering.

In a true marriage, people approach each other to build the temple of happiness. The temple was not there before. They are now called into duty to build it—to build it with their best thoughts, best feelings and best acts, in devotion, in culture, in sacrifice, and in respect.

They are now challenged to cultivate the seeds of beauty in each other, until the full flower radiates itself through their beings. They are now challenged to release the supreme values, the supreme lights in each other, cultivating each other as a gardener cultivates his garden, for only in progressive development can a couple fulfill their destiny.

To build the temple of joy and bliss, we need to use special instruments, and they must be always ready in our hands:

Freedom
Non-criticism
Admiration
Sacrifice
Education
Gratitude
Sense of responsibility.

Through these seven tools the temple can be built because they are the seven pillars of wisdom by which the temple is constructed.

What is *freedom?* It is very easy to explain. Our partner must have complete freedom to do, to feel, to think, in the way he or she thinks is proper. Only a free mate can be a true mate. The biggest touch-stone is freedom. Our partner is not our property. Our partner is a free being; he or she is there to build the temple of joy and understanding in the family as well. This temple can be built in mutual respect for each other's freedom. Neither should force his or her will upon the other. Freedom must be conditioned by the well-being and the highest goals of the family.

Freedom does not mean to exercise your desires or ideas upon another. In its true meaning, to be free means to express your inner light, love, and beauty through your own ways and means. To be free means to be released from all those thoughts, feelings and acts which are selfish, harmful, limiting, dark, separative, and destructive. A man who has achieved Soul consciousness is a free man because he is not the slave of his body, of his emotions, or of his thoughts and ideas.

The second tool is *non-criticism*. To criticize means to force your will upon another. We are not intended to make our partner the shadow of ourselves. Let us leave each person to bloom into his own flower, with his own original colors. Let us try to understand the motives, and be ready to help anytime we are asked for it. Let each one learn their own way.

The third tool is *admiration*. Let us show our admiration for each spark of light, love, and beauty expressed in our partner. Every time you admire a good deed, you increase the energy behind it. Admiration is like watering your garden. Admiration brings out your Soul Energy, and by a magnetic rapport releases the Soul Energy in your partner. Soul Energy creates more love, more joy, and more understanding. To admire means to see the highest in your partner.

The fourth tool is *sacrifice*. In its true meaning, to sacrifice means to destroy within ourselves those limiting forms, feelings, thoughts, and habits which prevent our progress toward deeper joy and understanding. These limitations may also prevent the blooming of our partner, so they must be sacrificed. In every act of sacrifice a new power operates within ourselves, and within our family. The ladder of progress is made by the steps of our every sacrifice.

Our fifth tool is *education*. We are intended to compliment each other, balance and release each other. We cannot do these things if we do not develop our physical, emotional, mental, and spiritual natures. We must have something to give, something to add. We must develop stronger and stronger wings if we want to fly toward the highest altitudes, to keep company with the flights of our partner. If one cannot share his higher joys, lights and admirations, the balance loses its equilibrium and the unity becomes weaker and weaker, until the one that is left behind loses his or her way, feeling lonely, depressed and miserable.

Our sixth tool is *gratitude*. It is the highest form of respect. To be grateful to each other means to appreciate and to recognize each other. To be grateful means to have in your consciousness all those good deeds, feelings, and thoughts that you enjoy in your partner. Let us be grateful for our friends, for our trees and flowers, for the smiles of our wife or husband, for the joys of our children. Let us appreciate life; let us feel the Divine Presence in everything and be grateful. Let us be grateful for the Will of God, and see the good in everything, and enjoy it with our full being. When we are being grateful, we release the constructive energies within ourselves and within the family. A grateful face always radiates joy, love, and light; such a person is a powerhouse for friends.

Our seventh tool is a *sense of responsibility*. This is the consciousness of being one with the other. To understand it simply, we can ask ourselves: "Do my words, acts, feelings or thoughts increase the happiness, the joy, the light, and the health of my partner, or decrease them? Do I know that everything good for my partner is good for me too? Do I know that I will pay the cost for all those words, deeds, feelings, and thoughts that retard or prevent the progress of my mate? Do I know that a small seed of evil can grow throughout centuries and block the door of light for myself and for others?"

Our sense of responsibility is the most important tool in our hand. Those who have it are the guardian angels of humanity.

We do not belong to ourselves; we belong to each other, to our family, race, nation, humanity, and even to the universe. We can help the well-being of the universe, or be an evil influence within it. With our sense of responsibility, we unite ourselves with the constructive forces, with the Forces of Light in the universe, and are blessed in our individual and family life.

Our sense of responsibility is the end of our selfish motives and egocentric activities.

Using these seven tools, and meditating upon them every day, we can build the temple of happiness, joy, and bliss in our families. If such families do increase in the world, humanity will enter into its true heritage of bliss; and the energy behind all of these is the Energy of Love.

When two advanced people are attracted by true love, the following things occur:

A. They establish magnetic lines of communication between their hearts.
B. Their auras start to merge into each other.
C. After their merging, the assimilation process starts when each one enriches the other's aura with his or her hues and vibrations.
D. The centers start to give corresponding signs of vibration, thus sublimation starts.
E. New energies awaken, precipitating new inspirations and light.
F. At the more advanced degrees of love, our physical, emotional, and mental levels are united, and Soul-fusion becomes a fact.
G. The couple starts to work for a great goal.

A lasting love between two people is not a ready made object. It does not come by chance, cannot be purchased or found. You have to plant it, look after it, protect and nurse it, and give it the needed soil, water, light, and energy. This takes time. The growth of love between two people can be compared to their ascent of a high mountain. They begin their journey on opposite sides of the mountain, but the higher they climb the closer they come to each other, until one day they meet on the peak of the mountain. To climb the mountain means to raise the level of your being and gradually clear your consciousness, enlarge your horizon of light and service, and enter into deeper levels of responsibility toward each other. Only through such a life is the path of love built.

So we may say that those who love each other deeply and sincerely are those people who meet more frequently, and more often walk together on the path of love toward the peak. So many people are climbing with us, and in every life we meet some of them. The paths toward the peak are in the form of spirals, and on every turn peoples paths cross. Let us call these crossroads our earthly marriages, and lives. For example, on one of the crossroads two people meet each other; they love each other and marry. After they pass the crossing point in the spiral they gradually get further and further apart, until again a crossroad comes and they meet. We cannot say that the same persons will meet each other again and again. It depends on how they walked, what speed they traveled, how they grew, how they lived, and how they reacted to each other.

This meeting at the many crossroads will continue in eternity, and as they get nearer the peak, the two persons will meet more frequently upon every crossroad. They will know each other immediately and will fall in love, on all levels. They will sacrifice themselves to each other, and do their best to make the life of the other more beautiful, glorious, and supreme.

The day will come when they will meet so often that after a period of time they will never separate, for they will reach the peak of love.

People speak about soul mates. There is no ready-made soul mate; however, we can build one with great labor and sacrifice over centuries and eternity. Once you meet the one on the top of the mountain, he or she is yours eternally. The two of you are one. In this unity of soul and spirit is hidden the glory of love.

The higher you climb, the deeper you breathe, and the deeper you radiate love.

The term "soul mate" is thought to apply only to husband and wife relationships. This is a limited concept.

Soul mates are not necessarily limited by physical relationships, or by sex. Soul mates can be sister and brother; or sister and sister; or a man and woman who have a deep feeling, understanding, and spiritual telepathy between each other.

Most of the soul mates are great workers in international projects in the field of world service, with great dedication and sacrifice. It is even possible that they can work simultaneously in a great project from both subjective and objective sides of nature.

Love is life; love is the song of the Absolute, and all manifestation is a harp through which He is expressing His love, playing His music. That is why the supreme duty of every creature is to love. Every time we really love we express that Divine Current, that Divine Song. Every time we act against love, we impede the divine circulatory flow; we break the harmony of His Music, of His Song, and cut ourselves from the energy of life and suffer in innumerable ways.

Saint Francis of Assissi wrote some beautiful lines about love. He said,

"Blessed is he that truly loves and seeketh not love in return; Blessed is he that serves and desires not to be served; Blessed is he that doeth good unto others and seeketh not that others do good unto him."

And Saint Paul summarized all these explanations in a most beautiful expression,

"Though I speak with the tongues of men and of angels, and have not love in my heart, I am become as sounding brass or a tinkling cymbal . . . Love is long-suffering and kind; love does not envy; love does not make a vain display of itself and does not boast . . . bears all things, believes all things, hopes all things, endures all things . . . And now abide faith, hope, love, these three; but the greatest of these is love."[2]

Chapter 8

LOVE IN ACTION

HEN WE SPEAK about love, we must emphasize that
it has two main functions:
1. Protection
2. Direction
Firstly, love can protect. When man is full of
love he uses his words, his actions, his thoughts, and his emotions
in a way that does not cause harm to, or hinder the evolution of
another man. Thus, love protects one from doing things that will
harm others. One thinks, feels, acts, and speaks motivated by
love for others.

The second function of love is to direct energy to a certain person. It is similar to turning on a switch of electrical current and
directing that energy toward a certain mechanism. Directive energy must be used with caution. It is fortunate that few people
know how to do this. Love energy channeled without discrimination can do great harm to those to whom it is directed. Not know-

161

ing how to handle it or because of their mental, emotional, or physical pollution, it can be used destructively, even against the one who channeled it to them.

Love is not emotion, although it can be found in our emotions. Love comes from our Inner Guide, or from our Intuitional plane. However, if our astral plane is not pure, this energy is used for personal satisfaction. For example, it is the release of Love Energy into a non-pure mechanism that creates *lust* or overactive sex. This leads to related complications, such as partisanship, leading to racial and national fanaticism and to related crimes. It leads to separative idealism and to related miseries—revolution and war. The reason for all of these aberrations is that the Love Energy, to a certain degree, is released in a mechanism which is filled with maya, glamor, illusions, prejudices, and superstitions.

When one's motives and heart are really purified but they do not use discrimination and wisdom in channeling Love Energy to those who are polluted by various contaminations, they can inadvertently increase the misery of those people as well as the misery of the world.

Love Energy is electrical, and it is always safeguarded by Wisdom. That is why the second major energy ray in the universe is called the Love-Wisdom Ray.

When one has love and lives in the Light of Love, through a life of goodwill, harmlessness, and creative service, it is possible to direct that Love Energy to those special people who need it for their heavy tasks and for their sacrificial services.

We must realize that a person full of love radiates it out naturally. This is normal. There is no danger in radiating love, since people will register it if they are sensitive to it, or are ready for it as a result of their karma. However, when love is deliberately directed, it may overflow the centers of the subject causing disturbances in them. This will activate or overstimulate their maya, glamors, and illusions and make them victims of these overflowing forces.

Pure Love Energy can be channeled discriminately when we are functioning on the Intuitional plane. This is a rare achievement. If one is below the Intuitional plane they must not attempt to send *Love Energy* to anyone, because that energy will be contaminated with their own glamors, illusions, and vices thus causing disturbances in the person to whom it was directed. We must use our love cautiously.

One day a young boy with a black eye came to me. I asked "What is wrong with your eye?"

"Love," he said, "love."

"What happened?"

"I was dancing with a girl last night and we had such good rapport that I wanted to kiss her to show my love. When I was just about to kiss her, she slapped my face and her ring hit my eye."

"What did you learn from this?"

"Do not love somebody who is not ready to love you."

Love can create hatred if it is not used with wisdom. The above mentioned girl did not necessarily hate that boy. But through her past experience and education she saw a danger in that act, and an irresponsible move in his action.

It is not your love that creates antagonism but the way you handle it and in the degree to which you use it.

I also remember a girl, a young girl full of love, who was asked by a man to help him sexually. The girl, because of her pity and the man's need, offered herself to him. A few days later she found she had contracted a venereal disease, and later discovered she was pregnant. When talking to me, she said, "Out of my love, I wanted to help him."

If she had had more discrimination, less pity, and had used her love to uplift that man into a higher level of thinking, other than offering sex to him, her love could have been used in a better way.

Love is not only a giving, but also a rejecting act; not only a going out, but also a withdrawal; not only an allowing act, but also a preventing act. It is not only gentle and sweet; but highly disciplinary. When a person is taking advantage of your love to satisfy his vices and criminal intentions, and to prevent your growth and evolution on the path, to cooperate with him will be equal to assenting to his crimes.

To "love your enemy" does not mean to encourage him in his destructive practices. One must take action to prevent those practices, for his sake and for the sake of others who may be involved in the practices of the "enemy."

A person taking action against his enemy may even save him and lead him into constructive living, or disarm him, and give him a chance to grow in 'understanding.' This takes courage, wisdom, decisiveness, insight, and a very real love.

However, if your enemy appears to be an enemy because he is revealing your transgressions, injustices and weaknesses, he is your friend in disguise. You need to love him and learn your lesson from him.

The rays of the sun create or affect plants according to their reactions. Similarly the Energy of Love creates effects according to the reactions and responses of a human being. If their nature is full of glamors, illusions, and vices, the Love Energy may multiply them just as the rays of the sun multiply the germs of trash that are exposed to the sun. That is why the vehicles of a human being must be purified before Love Energy is released to them.

Many psychological and physical diseases are the result of the contamination and pollution which we create in our atmosphere. When the pure life-giving rays are passing through the polluted atmosphere for many thousands of miles, their chemistry is changed, and when it hits the life on this planet it can create very unhealthy responses. In a sense because of our pollution, we are changing the life-giving influence of the Sun into a destructive influence. This will become more evident as the years pass by.

This is exactly the case with Love Energy. Unless it is directed through a pure atmosphere to a pure mechanism, or a striving mechanism with pure motive, your Love Energy will miss its mission.

The true Love Energy creates striving, self-exertion, a great urge and tendency towards purity and cooperation with the Plan. Unless there is total purity, there will be no spiritual unity. Cooperation is a step towards unity. Love is an urge to organize the life of the planet in accordance with the Will of God. Love is a fiery courage to make all men see the Divinity within each other and to work for each other's spiritual salvation.

Love, or that which man understands as love, has eight phases as shown below. In the future however, man may find different words to explain each phase.

1. Love for food and possessions.
2. Love of sex.
3. Love for family.

4. Love for race, group.
5. Love for nation.
6. Love for beauty, culture, friends, teacher, and Master.
7. Love for the Divine in all forms, in every man.
8. Cosmic Love.

Love is contact and fusion. Through each phase the human soul expands gradually and fuses itself with the Almighty Presence in all forms, solar systems, and galaxies.

It is only through the expanding process of love that love exists. This is a very important point to ponder upon. Love is just like a flame or fire; it exists only in burning brightly and in expanding.

Separated love can be called by various names—such as greed, selfishness, hatred, lust, fanaticism, nationalism, partisanship, racism. In short, any attitude that separates, possesses or enslaves, and does not grow into and allow freedom and does not expand toward the whole, is not love.

Loving is expansion. In loving we clear the obstacles on the path of all our relationships. Loving makes us feel that there is no end. Love is the door to Infinity.

Chapter 9

FREEDOM

HE MONADIC PLANE is the plane of freedom. Those who function in that plane are free souls, great souls. In that plane self-cognition and self-actualization are facts. This plane is the door through which the Initiate passes to cosmic evolution.

Each initiation is a great step toward freedom, a great step toward compassion and unity. Freedom is the path of individual, planetary, and cosmic evolution. And evolution is the process of "becoming oneself." Step by step the Inner Spark becomes Itself.

Evolution is the process of the liberation of the spirit from the prison of form. By this struggle for liberation the matter evolves and unfolds, producing more and more perfected mechanisms for the expression of the Inner Life. The phenomenal man is one of the mechanisms created through the process of liberation of the Spirit.

167

Evolution proceeds on three roads, or in a triple way:

A. We have the outer evolution, which is the evolution of the atom and the form.
B. We have the evolution of the Solar Angel.
C. We have the evolution of the Spirit, through liberations and individualization.

These three resemble three wheels. They all turn, but not at the same speed. Sometimes evolution A turns faster, sometimes B, and somtimes C.

From the point of view of the cosmos there is always progress, but from the human angle, when one or another slows down or speeds up, we think that evolution is zig-zagging. On the down side we call it degeneration, on the up side we call it progress. But this observation is from a narrow point of view of time and space. It is actually all progress.

Evolution A is the evolution of matter, also the evolution of astral and mental matter. All the tiny lives in all these three planes are evolving; this is an "unfolding of a continuously increasing power to respond."

Evolution B concerns the Thinker within us. It has Its own evolution. Also, It is an agent of evolution—serving as a center of communication between the higher and the lower.

It is our Solar Angel, or the Ego, which aeons ago redeemed Itself from the chains of matter and saw the glory of the Self within itself. Now It is working to unveil that Greater Beauty within itself through continuous meditation. In the meantime, It is trying to shed light on the tiny lives in the three bodies, and cause them to unfold—thus the human soul evolves.

Evolution C is the evolution of the human soul which is the "fallen" Spark going back Home. Man is in the process of becoming a soul, and then his Real Self, the Spark. The evolving human soul, the unfolding Spark, senses its true picture in the Spark or Ego. For a while that Spark is its Home.

Afterwards, when the human reaches the level of a Soul, it will see its own jewel within itself.

Conscious evolution starts when the evolving human soul starts to respond to the light of the Inner Thinker, and obeys consciously the pure ideas projected by the Great Beings.

Our planetary life is a center in the Greater Life of the Sun. This Greater Life expresses Itself through seven planes. These planes are formed of tiny lives. Each life is progressing toward the Central Spiritual Sun. Man is a cell in the "body" of that Greater Being, Greater Life. That Greater Life is progressing; so are all the tiny lives and forms on the planet. This is unconscious evolution. There is no freedom in unconscious evolution.

Freedom begins when you start to become yourself, a conscious cell in that Greater Life. You become a co-worker for the Great Purpose toward which that Greater Life is progressing. The further you respond to the Purpose of that Greater Life, the more freedom you obtain and the greater service you render. Beauty becomes your life expression, and goodness your light.

Conscious evolution is a process of awakening, and an increasing response to the higher ideas, to the Plan and to the Purpose of our Solar Logos. No freedom is possible in sleep, and no man starts to awaken unless he starts to respond consciously to the Light of the Thinker within him.

Actually, every step toward the Self is a step toward freedom.

Freedom is not a physical condition. Freedom is not an escape from our responsibilities and duties. Freedom is an Inner Radioactivity from which beauty, goodness, and truth shine out and spread life everywhere, in spite of all physical, emotional, and mental obstacles. In such a state of freedom a prisoner can be the freest one, and a ruling king can be the most miserable slave.

The energy of freedom is the propelling power behind all creation. It is the energy behind all cultures and civilizations. It exists in each of us. It is the atmosphere in which the Real Self lives. That is why we cannot enjoy or experience full freedom until we become our Real Self.

Once you experience the energy of freedom you become a living fire. When the ancients were keeping the fire perpetual; when they were worshiping the light, the lightning, the sun; when they were placing that fire upon their altars, they were actually worshiping the energy of freedom, the Source of freedom.

This state of freedom is the result of conscious evolution, the result of long ages of suffering, detachment, and observation. Nothing in nature can easily be achieved. The path to freedom is hard work. On this path the petals of freedom slowly unfold and spread the fragrance of love, sincerity, respect, gratitude, harmlessness, sense of responsibility, creativity, service, sacrifice.

Sometimes people think that a man who has a deep sense of responsibility and an intense will-to-serve, is a slave. This is not true. The sense of responsibility and the will-to-serve are the first major signs that a man is now able to detach himself from the chains of selfish interests; is able to refuse hindrances coming from his physical, emotional, and mental natures; is able to reject any personality response to the surrounding condition; and is now able to remain in the peace of the Soul, trying to live intelligently for the welfare of humanity.

Man's slavery starts when he begins to live for himself and forgets his responsibilities. This leads him into physical and psychological disorders, or chains. You cannot escape from your debts except by paying them.

We overcome our little self by living for others. And if we are doing this wisely, we call it sense of responsibility. As our sense of responsibility gets clearer and deeper, our true value appears because we release the hidden light within us, which is our true SELF.

We have three thick walls around us:

The first wall is the inertia of the body, or the chaos of blind urges and drives in our etheric body.

We have the thick wall of our glamors, for example:

"The glamor of being busy."
"The glamor of conflict, with the objective of imposing righteousness and peace."
"The glamor of materiality, or over-emphasis of form."
"The glamor of adherence to forms and persons."
"The glamor of the mysterious and the secret."[1]

We also have the wall of the chaos of illusion in our mental plane. Illusion is created when the developing human soul starts to work on the mental plane, where many waves of ideas and thoughtforms are found. Because of his inexperience and the lack of clarity of vision he cannot see these ideas and thoughtforms as they are. He tries to translate them, interpreting them incorrectly, and thus creates illusions. That is why a man becomes more dangerous when he starts to function on the mental plane, and sometimes becomes more confused in his life.

This creation of illusion continues until the evolving human soul expands his consciousness toward the Greater Light Within, the Solar Angel, and starts to see things as they are on the mental plane.

Each illusion is a hindrance to freedom. Before a man steps to higher levels of the mental plane or enters into the freedom of the Intuitional plane, he must cleanse himself of all his illusions—through meditation and acts of goodwill.

The Tibetan Master refers to another great obstacle on the path toward freedom. He calls it "the dweller on the threshold." This also is a thick wall, a big thoughtform, built by the blind urges and drives of the etheric body, by the glamors of the emotional nature and by the illusions of the mental nature. A man who lives in the midst of these blind urges, glamors, and illusions cannot say that he is a free man. Such a man is a machine. He is in a state of dreaming, and any outer stimulus may create an unconscious response from the mechanism.

Freedom is a state of awareness. In that state your true Self is not conditioned by any formula, doctrine, dogma, expression or by any physical, emotional, or mental form. You can penetrate through them and see things as they are.

Freedom is obedience to cosmic principles. Only through such obedience can you destroy your limitations and hindrances. *Obedience* has an esoteric meaning. On the path to freedom *obedience* becomes a ladder; upon each step the traveler rejects the lower and accepts the higher.

Conscious obedience is a process of recognition and assimilation of the Greater Ideas which are projected toward the human world as guide lights on the path to freedom. They represent the true authority, the true experience. Man cannot reject them and be free. On the contrary, his freedom is achieved by the recognition of authority and experience, and by his identification with them.

The goal of the cell is to obey the direction of the Central Life. The goal of all the tiny lives of our three worlds—and up—is to let the Will of the Inner Spark radiate through them. This is the meaning of obedience.

When the cells or atoms resign their tiny wills and subject themselves consciously to the Higher Will of the Inner Self, they have the possibility of being released from their limiting walls, and of stepping into the freedom of a Higher Will. Cosmic Intentions are sensed by and impressed upon the higher levels of the Spiritual Triad, and only Great Souls can enter there, bring them out and translate them for us.

The teachings of great Souls such as Buddha, Krishna, Zoroaster, and Christ were formulations of such Cosmic Intentions. Beauty, goodness, truth, love, unity, purity, and sacrifice—these are seven paths which lead us into the Source of Cosmic Principles. Each step toward that Source is a step toward freedom. Acts against these Cosmic Intentions are steps toward slavery. A slave is a man who obeys his body, glamors, and illusions or he obeys the bodies, glamors, and illusions of his environment. He swims in the ocean of such slavery, and he calls it freedom.

A free man is a man who tries to dispel attachment to matter, to the body, to the blind urges. He tries to dispel the glamors and illusions of the society. He tries to eliminate the chains which were created through the attachment to matter, through glamor and separativeness. Such a man is a benefactor of the human race. He wants to find the causes of sickness, the causes of social misery, wars, hatred, revolution, ignorance and slavery, and eliminate them.

Such a man who wants to be free and to free others from such social hindrances strongly disciplines his body, cleanses his emotional world, and sharpens his mind. Only through such techniques can he reach the land of freedom and lift others toward that freedom. A musical artist cannot release the fire of his genius on an untuned violin. Great principles can only work out if the vehicles of expression are in the highest order of discipline and purity. Only through discipline and purity can one reach freedom. Actually the whole message of Christ is a message of freedom. The whole message of Buddha, Krishna, and Zoroaster are the messages of freedom. And all those who sacrificed their lives for such freedoms are heroes of the New Age—the Age of Freedom.

In the New Age the process of freedom is the process of appropriation, of fitting, of cooperation, of sharing, of right human relations with higher and lower dimensions. Actually, freedom is not isolation. On the contrary, the highest freedom is total communication. Whenever you have a communication gap, that is your obstacle to freedom. Erase that obstacle and you are more free.

A synthesizing process is progress toward freedom. A separative process is a path toward slavery. Total freedom is freedom for the whole human race. No man can really achieve total freedom as long as slavery exists in the world; slavery of the body, emotions, and mind.

Those who once are charged with the energy of freedom themselves become liberators on all levels. That is why they face the pressure of slavery; the hate and destructive forces of the physical, emotional, and mental slaves.

In sacrificing our lives for others, we are building the great temple of freedom. In using others for our little self, we are creating a prison for ourselves. In sharing we become more free; in hoarding we limit ourselves. In hating we are isolating ourselves; in loving we are becoming universal, even cosmic.

Freedom is the name of an energy which detaches us from limitations, pushes us into right human relations, into more sharing, into more communication and synthesis. The highest freedom is total sacrifice, and total sacrifice is absolute communication.

The Real Self is the fountain of the energy of freedom. That is why in the process of becoming oneself man progressively enters into more freedom, until he is released into the total freedom of his SELF.

Beauty, goodness, and truth are synthesized in freedom. But man cannot experience freedom until he expresses beauty, goodness, and truth in his total life. Any act against beauty, goodness, or truth leads a man into slavery.

A free man is highly charged with energy. He is a man who releases you physically, emotionally, mentally, and spiritually because he creates in you harmony, integration, contact with higher levels, and health.

Health is freedom; sickness is slavery. Health is harmony; sickness is chaos. Harmony is freedom. Knowledge is freedom. Ignorance is slavery.

Increasing knowledge is increasing freedom. Slavery starts when the knower stops knowing more, when the lover stops loving more, when the server stops serving more. Freedom is the expansion of the Essence; slavery is the expansion of the *form* instead of the Essence.

Materialism is slavery. Totalitarianism is a big prison. A true disciple of wisdom rejects both materialism and totalitarianism in all their expressions in any field. A true disciple stands for freedom.

Franklin Delano Roosevelt was a great disciple who formulated the four essential freedoms:

Freedom of speech
Freedom of worship
Freedom from want
Freedom from fear

These were given to humanity on January 6, 1941. A few months later, on August 14, 1941, another page of the gospel of freedom was given to humanity in the form of the Atlantic Charter. And later, another page was given in the form of the Declaration of Human Rights.

It is now the time for people to learn to discriminate and not support those movements which are planning violence, and working against the integrity of our economic, social, and cultural life.

Our country stands on the foundation of the spirit of freedom. But freedom does not mean freedom to exploit, brainwash, or impose one's own will on others.

Freedom means to live in such a way that others have a greater chance to enjoy the blessings of life, and choose their own ways to live, their own ways to worship and their own ways to create. We know that man has no right to hurt any human being, but we have not yet learned that man has no right to hurt himself either.

Drugs, alcohol, unhealthy sex, and other unwholesome activities cannot be tolerated even on a personal basis, because the effect of any personal action is shared by all of us in one way or another.

No one has the right to say, "I can do anything I want to do with myself."

True freedom is the ability to choose the wisest way to act, to feel, to think, so that you increase the chance of survival, success and prosperity of all that exists.

The new world religion will have a major key. That key will be freedom. It will be the gospel of beauty, goodness, and truth.

Chapter 10

JOY

I

". . . joy is a special wisdom."[1]

N THE HIGHER REALMS of the mental plane there is an energy center which resembles a lotus, or a chalice, radiating many colors when it is in full bloom.

Joy is the fragrance of the chalice, the lotus. As the petals of the lotus unfold, joy radiates out of the petals and gives vigor to the physical body, magnetism to the subtle body, and serenity to the mental body.

The lotus is the permanent source of joy. As it unfolds joy increases. Joy is not conditioned by outer circumstances; it is like a beacon, the foundation of which rests on the ageless rocks.

Happiness is an effect of outer conditions. When favorable conditions change, happiness disappears, leaving the gloom of depression.

Joy never changes. It increases as the problems and conflicts increase in one's life. It grows in spite of conditions. As the experience of the pilgrim increases, as the field of his service expands, as he wills to sacrifice more and more, as he conquers more territory in self-realization, the fragrance of the lotus increases and spreads over vaster areas.

The most attractive energy of a server is his joy, which radiates from his manners, from his voice, and through his eyes. Whatever he touches blooms and unfolds.

Joy is not a feeling, nor is it an emotion; it is a state of consciousness, a state which is detached from the domination of the three lower worlds. The problems of these three worlds cannot reach it. Knowledge, love, and the dynamic energy of the sacrificial petals are spread out and they charge all the tiny lives of the lower vehicles with the energy of joy.

Joy is not the absence of hindrances, problems and difficulties. On the contrary, joy is the flash springing out of each victory earned by the inner man through these obstacles. Joy grows in battle, in conflict, in service, in sacrifice. Real joy creates crises and tensions, and overcomes them. This is how joy grows. Joy overcomes all hostilities, all doubt, and builds numberless bridges between the hearts.

Joy gives courage, inspiration and vision. It purifies, heals and sanctifies.

In the light of a joyful man, people see themselves as they are. All shadows of doubt disappear. They become inspired by a greater vision. The energy of courage starts to flow through their nerves. They make difficult decisions while joy enflames their hearts toward greater beauties. Joy uplifts them and makes them more able, more free, and more radioactive. No one can hurt you if joy is there. Black arrows from visible or invisible worlds fall down in front of the fortress of joy. Joy is harmony; that is why the black arrows cannot penetrate it.

Any attack against joy produces depression, gloom, darkness, failure in the attacker. Any communication with joy uplifts, exalts, and beautifies.

Joy is the alchemical stone. It is the Path to Life, to Love, to Light. It is the magnetism of the Sun.

Locked doors and fenced paths open to the presence of joy.

You can understand the expression of joy in any language. From any level you can translate it into your own.

A joyful man is the simplest man, the most straightforward man and the most profound man. You always understand him, but always you find something deeper in him. When you penetrate one depth, another depth reveals itself. Through the simplicity of joy you are led into the mysteries of joy.

Success is the result of a labor which is carried on in joy. Start your work with joy and the path of success will open in front of you. Communicate with joy, work with joy. Be joyful in all of your relationships, and even observe your failures with joy, in joy. Any failure observed in joy changes itself into success and victory. Any problems observed in joy dissolve. Joy is for Infinity. Joy is for changelessness. And joy is the witness of the imperishability of the human flame.

The form of the warriors' salutation for the New Age will be, "*Rejoice!*"

This is not a handshake, nor a hello. This is not a kiss, or an embrace. It is an act of charging people with the energy of joy. It is an act of uplifting them from the waves of the three worlds and holding them in beauty, in gratitude, in courage, in hope, in vision, and in reality.

"*Rejoice!*" Joy is the fragrance rising out of the Inner Chalice, an ever singing melody.

In great humility, in great simplicity, enter into the Inner Sanctuary and see the chalice. Look at the flame in the chalice, the fire of bliss. Place your lips on the chalice and taste it. Then enter into the ecstasy of love, of joy, of bliss.

JOY

II

WITHIN EACH HUMAN BEING there is the "memory of Home." The memory of Home is a very beautiful memory, a feeling that once upon a time the "Spark" or the Spirit within our hearts was part of the "Sun," was part of the omnipotent, omnipresent, and omniscient Existence from which it was projected out into space as a Ray and eventually was trapped in the world of matter, emotion, and mind.

The Home was total bliss or beatitude, the memory of which still remains in our hearts as the hope and path on which we will return Home. Thus each Spark of life has the urge to be happy, to be in joy, in bliss.

We feel that our present state is not the state we want to be in. We do not have a state of permanent satisfaction, so we want something different, something more, and we do not yet clearly know what it is we are searching for. There is a faint memory of it, and in rare moments of happiness, joy and bliss, we feel we are approaching Home.

All that we want to do, all that we want to be in the world, is to be happy, to be full of joy, full of bliss, or to be bliss. All the rest are ways and means to reach the Source of our memory.

In the Upanishads it says, 'TAT TVAM ASI.' YOU ARE THAT. You are the supreme bliss in your Essence. Your Self is part of that Life from which all things proceeded.

It is very interesting that, blinded by our ignorance and material life we search for the *bliss* in our physical happiness, in our emotional pleasures, in our plans and logic, in the dollar, in possessions and positions, in diplomas, in our ranks and titles . . . and after searching and attaining all that we want, we realize that the real joy and real bliss is not found in them . . . and we ask, "Where can I find satisfaction for my thirsty heart?"

The answer is given to us by the sages of all ages, "The bliss

178

is within you, the bliss is you. Meet yourself, be yourself and you will find the answer to your questions."

When our consciousness is focused within our physical, emotional or mental natures, we are always in fear. There are three main areas where our consciousness can be focused in the physical, emotional, or mental realms:

1. Personality consciousness sees things as they appear. It is conditioned by death, disintegration, sickness, loss, loneliness, pain, by various needs, by the things you want to have and you do not have, by things you have but you lose. It is based on *fear, greed, hatred, anger.*

Often our happiness is based upon a successful business, but we see that it does not last forever. Things happen and the business goes wrong. Many great businesses were destroyed by an earthquake, by an epidemic, by a hurricane, by death of certain executives, by war or by revolution. Happiness based on things that are not permanent have always carried the seeds of sorrow and misery.

2. When we are identified with our emotional pleasures or emotional objects, we feel happy. But then we experience bitterness and pain when we lose our emotional objects with their pleasures. We eventually learn that there is no permanent happiness in our emotional objects, because they come and go with mixed pleasures and inherent sorrows. But the search continues. No matter how much disappointment life gives us, we keep searching for happiness and gradually turn to a higher level of existence.

3. We begin to search for our happiness within the mental realms. The mental objects catch our attention because we see that there is more stability and permanency in the mental plane than on the previous two planes, the physical and emotional.

In the mental plane some of us search for our happiness in daydreams, in religion, philosophy or ideology, but eventually we find that these also do not give us the satisfaction or joy for which we were looking.

When we are identified with our thoughtforms, with our religion, philosophy, or ideology we are always in a state of fear of losing them. Such a fear leads us into destructive actions in which are found the seeds of sorrow and pain. The destiny of fanatics of all ages is a witness to this fact.

A fanatic is a man who is identified with his religion or his racial or national superstitions, which eventually become a burden on his back and the source of his suffering.

There is also a tendency to search for joy and bliss in high positions or careers. It is possible to have temporary joy in mental objects, in mental interests, but eventually we find out that it is possible to be a lawyer but not necessarily a happy person; it is possible to be a doctor but not necessarily a healthy person; it is possible to be a space scientist but not necessarily a contented person. It is possible to be the president of a great nation, but be loaded by heavy guilt feelings or frustration.

The pursuit of happiness in all these fields ends with disappointment. In the final analysis we find that we had drops of joy only in those creative moments when we tried to serve, to uplift, and bring joy to others during our search for happiness in our physical, emotional, and mental objects.

I was talking with a heart surgeon when he was close to death. He said, "I am dying unhappy because all that I did was blindly motivated to collect millions of dollars. I married a very beautiful woman who was the wife of my best friend, then I divorced her because I found a younger girl who died in an accident. Now everything ends in tragedy . . . my wealth goes to my children who dope themselves day and night."

One thing I could say to him, "You will have more chances to search for your joy in the more permanent values of life in another cycle."

Our physical, emotional, and mental happiness is intensified when we integrate our personality vehicles—our physical, emotional, and mental nature—and enjoy our sunny days as a united mechanism.

Thus the man's integrated personality is internally content, but is subject to those outside conditions which are related to his physical, emotional, and mental life.

Man is like a boat on the ocean. He enjoys a few sunny days and then is caught by wind, rain, or snow. Then he alternately passes through dark and sunny days. His happiness always has a short life.

When man's personality is healthy and in a state of satisfaction with what he has, with what he feels, and with what he knows and is, the man feels an intense happiness.

Many personalities were temporarily happy in the ocean of their physical possessions, emotional pleasures, and mental interests. But when the storms came, they lost all that they had, because their treasure was carried in the boat of the personality.

Happiness is related to the personailty and the first phase of the search for bliss is carried on in the field of personality, in which only a faint flash of happiness exists.

Buddha once said, "Everything is suffering—birth is suffering, life is suffering, death is suffering." The reason for this suffering is that man is identified with his physical, emotional, and mental interests.

One must pass through such experiences of dissatisfaction on the personality level before he starts to search for the bliss somewhere else. The disappointment of the personality as a whole causes a new breakthrough on a new dimension.

I knew an extremely beautiful twenty-one year old girl but had not seen her for twenty years. One day a middle-aged woman visited me and said, "Do you know me?"

I answered, "Your eyes are familiar, but I do not remember where we met or what your name is."

She looked like a witch; her face was wrinkled, her eyes blackened, her hair was in a desperate condition and she smelled heavily of liquor. She said, "I am very unhappy, don't you remember me? I am B . . ."

"I can't believe my eyes."

"Yea," she said, "I am ugly, right?"

"My goodness!"

She fell into my arms and began to cry.

"What happened to you? Why didn't you contact me?"

"I don't know. I want to die."

"Why?"

"Because I lost my beauty; and because I lost my beauty I lost my friends; and because I lost my friends I lost my job."

"You can be beautiful again."

"With such a face?"

"Beauty is not in our face or in our body; beauty is in our hearts, our souls, in our ideas, dreams, in our sacrificial service, in Christ.

You can be beautiful again if you look for it—not in your personality, but in your Soul. When the Soul shines, even the rocks radiate beauty."

"Can I find my happiness again?"

"You don't need to be happy, you need to be joyful."

"Joyful?"

"Yes, joyful. To find joy you will search not in the places where you were looking, but beyond your personality—in your Inner Core."

"You never changed," she noticed. "How come you do not hate me in this shape?"

"You are always beautiful, and because you are now disappointed, a new path is opening in front of you."

No one can really advance in a higher search if the foundation on which he stands is not shaken and destroyed. You need a crisis to make a breakthrough. The wind and the storm must come and hit your existence and test your foundation. Is your foundation based on your bank account, on your present health, on your position, on your friends? All these can be taken from you in one storm if your foundation is not built on your spiritual achievements and realizations. If your foundation is built on the solid rock of the transpersonal Self within you, no power can destroy it. Only in the Soul-awareness do you taste the beauty of joy.

First you were a boat; now you are a spaceship soaring into space, free from the destructive effects of waves, storms, lightning, clouds, and earthquakes.

A conscious Soul is an indestructible beauty and joy. Thus, the next stage in the search for bliss is Soul consciousness. This is the stage when joy starts. You are in the Soul and your realization is different. Instead of being subject to fear, anger, hate, and greed you are in the domain of a new consciousness, the main characteristics of which are:

Love
Immortality
Service
Joy
Contact with the Hierarchical Plan
Creativity.

Love is the ability to identify oneself with the life-aspect of manifestation.

Immortality is the realization that one was, one is, and will always be an individual existence. Immortality cannot be thought, but can be experienced. It is the result of spiritual achievement.

A characteristic of the transpersonal Self is love; a love that is given without expectation and anticipation. As you give more love you have more joy. Expectation relates you to personality levels.

Service is the ability to put into all your activities the solar fire of love, and the fire of the Plan. The Plan can be contacted in the Soul levels. It is an experience, not a teaching. The Plan is the map which shows you how to return to the Sun from which you were radiated out. The Plan is the map which shows you how to release yourself from the trap of your physical, emotional, and mental bodies and achieve the state of awareness which you had originally.

All human endeavors are efforts to escape the prisons that we built or the prisons that others built for us. All human labor is the effort to escape the conditions which we hate. The Plan shows the way out of our prisons.

Service is the ability to express the fire of the Plan through all that we think, feel, speak, and do.

In the Soul consciousness we have the first experience of true joy. Joy is the realization that a man is no longer vulnerable; that he can lose nothing; that greater achievements are waiting for him; that he can lift some people to the level of Soul consciousness where they taste the true joy; that, now he can see things as they are, not as they appear.

Unless we achieve Soul consciousness, we cannot understand the true meaning of invulnerability.

"Weapons cannot hurt the Self, nor fire burn It. Water cannot drench It, nor can wind make It dry. It cannot be divided. It is eternal and all pervading."[2]

Such an experience can be achieved in Soul consciousness. As you go deeper in joy you get closer to yourself. In joy, man has the realization that he can lose nothing.

In school we had a very beautiful teacher. He had the habit of taking his golden watch out of his pocket and putting it on the table. One day he came back and asked whether anyone saw his watch. The students said, "No." He was my best teacher, and I felt angry that anyone would take his watch and I went to him and said, "Who do you think may have stolen it from you?"

"It is not stolen," he said.

"Then," I asked, "What happened to it?"

"Somebody is using it."

I couldn't understand the secret of his behavior; he always had a great flow of joy in all his expressions. He was a joyful person.

In this event, my teacher gave me a chance to glimpse that in a certain state of consciousness you do not lose anything, because in Soul consciousness you do not possess anything.

Once Christ said, "Do not be afraid of those who try to kill you, but of those who try to kill your Soul."

Do not be afraid of those who try to attack your shadow, but be cautious of those who try to destroy your spiritual principles, your visions, your virtues, your values.

Joy gives a person a realization that greater achievements are waiting for him in the future. The vision of the future is an ever-growing joy in our hearts.

In Soul-consciousness, no matter what your personality life is passing through, there is a tomorrow, there is a new dawn, because the Soul is not limited by the failures of time, space, and matter. Even the failures of the personality can be utilized as firewood for the bonfire of the Soul.

The greatest failure of a man is contained in his actions that are directed against the Law of Love.

Joy offers a man the innate conviction that he can lift someone to the level of joy and make him joyful.

Once I was helping a young boy who was using drugs heavily. Eventually the boy overcame his habit and took up running, and began to study and to work. After being convinced that this was a permanent change in his being, I felt great joy. I went to my private room and asked myself, "Why are you so joyful?" "Oh my, a great burden is gone from my shoulders." "What burden?" "The burden of the usage of drugs."

Every time we help someone, we help ourselves. In Soul-consciousness the fragrance of joy radiates when you engage yourself in a labor of helping others without conditions.

In Soul-consciousness you have the eye to see things as they are, and not as they appear to be. When a man takes appearance as reality, he is caught in change. Joy is changelessness—in change.

It is told that the Law of Change is ever ruling. This is true for the world of phenomena, but it is not true for the world of Spirit. We lose our state of changelessness and are caught in the changing phenomena of life as we identify ourselves with the vehicles of our personality.

In Soul-consciousness, man comes in contact with the plan of his life, and eventually penetrates into the Plan of the Hierarchy for humanity. It is very interesting to note that the plan of our life is found in our Soul, and the Plan for humanity is found in the Hierarchy. Having a contact with the Plan, a man becomes a co-worker of great Servers of the human race. The Plan is formulated in such a way that it works for the welfare of humanity and for the welfare of each human being.

A Soul-conscious man tries to bring the Plan into daily life to help everyone, in every way, in everything so that he may be able to lead people from personality prisons to Soul-freedom, where they can experience the joy.

The next characteristic of the Soul is creativity. There is a great joy in creativity, because creativity is the process of letting the energies of the Plan flow and nourish the Sparks of Infinity in each living form.

In the presence of really joyful persons, people bloom. Joy is energy, and this energy nourishes the higher centers of human beings with the substance of higher mental fire. Then the hidden seeds of goodness, beauty, and truth come to life in them.

Joy does not stimulate lower centers, because it has a special high frequency which cannot be picked up by the lower centers. Joy does not overstimulate lower centers.

After a man proves that he can live in joy, be an embodiment and a fountain of joy, he is allowed to penetrate into the sphere in which bliss and ecstasy are found. That sphere in esoteric language is called the "Spiritual Triad."

Once I heard that there was a man in the Far East who was an advanced human being. I had a great desire to see him. When I finally located his retreat, his students told me that I could not see him because he was in meditation. I pretended that I was not interested in seeing him any more, but found a way to go to his room where he was sitting in meditation. He was in ecstasy. There was a peace in his room which you could almost touch. His face was radiating light and beauty.

I went a little closer and I felt a fiery energy on my skin. It was a burning joy. I went closer and closer, until I sat by him. A few minutes later my eyes were closed and I was nowhere. I only felt a great joy, bliss, and at-one-ment with all that exists. When my consciousness returned to its normal level I said to myself, this is bliss, it is a state of awareness in which you transcend time, space, and matter.

After anchoring myself on the mental plane I slowly went again into the blissful state in which I received unverbalized directions. I do not know how long I was in that state. I felt an arm around my shoulder and neck. I opened my eyes and looked into his eyes. For the first time in my life I saw Infinity. His eyes were doors leading to Infinity.

He did not talk. He hugged me and gave me a big smile. I went towards the door facing him, continuously looking at him.

In the Spiritual Triad we contact bliss. And it is from bliss that beauty radiates.

The Spiritual Triad is the domain of Infinity, where there is synthesis, there is Purpose, there is Will.

There are seven enemies of joy:

The first enemy is any action that causes or generates *fear* in other persons. Where there is fear the bird of joy flies away.

The second enemy is *anger*. Any time you act in anger it deprives you of your joy. Anything you do to make others angry takes the real joy of life from your heart. Anger may satisfy your emotions, but not your heart.

The third enemy of joy is *greed*. Whenever you have greed in your heart you lack joy. Greed is symbolized by a bottomless grave which never can be satisfied with human corpses. The most unhappy people are greedy people. Their happy moments are only secured by liquor, or by short moments of pleasure. Even in those moments of pleasure they feel the fear of losing it. I have seen many families fall apart because of the greed of the father, who was so occupied by making money that he would almost forget that he had a family.

The fourth enemy of joy is *hatred*. Any person who has hatred in his heart, or any group or nation which is polluted by hatred, will never taste the sunshine of joy, neither in the present nor in the future.

Joy is the connecting consciousness which makes you realize that you are one with everything.

Hatred is the feeling of separativeness. With hatred you cut many electrical lines within your system and within the international system, and when you turn off the switch of joy you have neither joy nor light. It is very interesting to notice that in joy, your light increases. You have purer discrimination and a better sense of values. In hatred your light decreases and your sense of altruistic values is almost nil.

Let us remember that actions performed in fear, anger, hatred, and greed create much bad karma on our path.

In Soul-consciousness there is love. Love purifies you and leads you into the fiery sphere of the Spiritual Triad. And in the awareness of that fiery sphere you taste the mighty bliss which you had when you were still one with the undivided space. That bliss was an unconscious bliss, and now your labor is to reach that bliss with your own effort and in your own right.

The fifth enemy of joy is *ugliness*. I was visiting a family and the man brought a birthday gift to a child six years of age. He made the child so excited with his gift that the boy was impatient to open the box. When the box was opened, a creature was found in it; a creature with a square head with horns, one eye looking east, the other eye looking west, ears hanging like bananas, legs tall and skinny like dry branches, one arm was fat, one boney. It was an embodiment of real ugliness.

"Hey," I exclaimed, "don't give that ugly creature to that boy, you will distort his imagination. Remove that ugliness." Why couldn't he bring something beautiful, something that would inspire the boy and give him joy?

A movie producer said that crime brings more money than any other kind of film. "Yes," I told him, "It may do so, but where will you hide when crime increases around you?"

"Until then," he answered, "I will have plenty of money to go somewhere else!"

Ugliness brings money, but not joy.

When the producer was ready to leave in his car, he loaded a gun and sat on it. "My goodness," I thought, "He is in fear already."

The sixth enemy of joy is *any action that is not based on goodwill.* Such an action takes your joy away from you.

The seventh enemy of joy is *any action that is not based on truth.* Lies take away your joy.

Ultimately joy is truth, beauty, and goodness. It is the ability to stand within the Soul-consciousness.

How can we climb to that level of Soul-consciousness?

1. Through *meditation on virtues.* In meditation we withdraw ourselves from fear, hatred, greed, anger, and from their consequences and connections, and stand in the light of our Inner Guide.

2. Through *causal thinking* because it liberates us from being caught in the phenomenal world. Causal thinking is the ability to penetrate into the roots of events, or to find the originating Cause instead of being stuck in the results and effects.

3. Through *living a life of beauty* in all our expressions.

A great Sage speaking about joy says, ". . . It is useful to impregnate space with joy. . . . Joy is the health of the spirit."[3]

The first step towards joy is *scientific meditation,* through which you eventually achieve Soul-infusion. Scientific meditation is an effort to penetrate into the mind of the real *Thinker,* which is the *Soul.* This is the transpersonal Self—or the Inner Guide.

In scientific meditation you begin to control, to discipline and to clear your mind so that it totally obeys your commands, and does not become a victim of the thoughts or suggestions coming from other minds.

There is a serious sickness in the world. We can call that sickness "abandonment of the boat." People allow other people to use their mental boat through hypnotism, suggestions, force, through bribery and various influences. As long as our minds do not belong to us we cannot *think,* and if we cannot *think,* those people who think through us will control us.

The Teaching tells us that we must not allow other minds to rule our mind. We must use our own mind, learn how to think; and meditation is the first step toward that freedom.

Joy abides with those who know how to think. Thinking leads

us to freedom. Thinking is the only means to escape imprisonment of the Spirit in any form. Thus on the path of joy we learn how to think, how to meditate.

Self-actualization cannot be achieved when other people use your mind. Your mind is your steering wheel; when other people have control over your steering mechanism you have no way of knowing where they are leading you.

The second step towards joy is *questioning*. Daily events, national events, and international events do not exist without causes. Ask yourself the reasons why these events took place. Develop observation of the causes. Try to see the cause behind every event. This will reveal to you many laws, principles, motives, and intentions hidden behind many relationships and activities. Understanding the causes will help you to direct your steps 'goal-fittingly.'

Try to consider the cause, not the manifestation. Do not react to the effects, but to causes whenever possible. Self-deception descends on us when we occupy ourselves with the phenomena and forget about causes, or the reasons why.

When you continue searching for the cause of events you will eventually develop double leveled sight, which reads the line, and also reads between the lines of the events.

The third step is to *live a life of beauty*; beauty in our personality, home, speech, manners, behavior, relationships; beauty in our emotional responses, thoughts, ideas, visions, and expressions. As we express beauty, the fire of joy increases in our vehicles and radiates out warming the hearts of others. The true joy manifests through beauty because joy is the expression of the Soul. Bliss is the expression of the Self.

Joy opens people's hearts, they talk and confess to you when they see there is abundant joy within you. Joy builds communication lines and gives strength and leads you to success. Any labor started and continued in joy will be a successful labor.

Joy never threatens people. They feel safe in the presence of a joyful man, because a joyful man is above personality interests. His nature is love.

Try joyfully to release; joyfully to resign and detach; joyfully to pay your bills. Joyfully renounce and joyfully live if you want your life to be a blessing for the world.

A great Sage speaking about joy says, ". . . . abysses have been crossed through joy and trust. Not only courage, but precisely joy makes you invulnerable."[4]

Also, "The manifestation of joy is accompanied by intensification of the work of the centers. Many attainments are accomplished by the manifestation of joy."[5]

Fear creates doubt. Doubt wastes energy. Joy annihilates fear. Joy increases our daring. One is daring when there is no fear in his heart.

Psychological dark moments of life can be crossed only through joy. Joy keeps your engine running. Joy gives clarity of vision to your mind. Fear, depression, and doubt poison our blood and the brain, and the mind cannot see things as they are. A poisoned bloodstream is the cause of most of our failures and ill-judgment.

Joy creates radioactivity in our aura, which repels all unworthy thoughts and negative emotions and builds a shield around the body. A joyful heart cannot be wounded by the flying arrows of the dark forces.

The etheric centers are intensified by joy, because joy is the fire of the Soul, and its flame creates radioactivity in the centers and synchronizes their rhythms. Thus, higher joy expands the fiery spheres of higher centers, which puts the consciousness of man in contact with higher planes. These are the moments of new realizations and new insights. New achievements are accomplished because of such contact and insights.

The flame of joy is the fire which emanates from the center of the chalice, from the center of the twelve petaled lotus in the higher mind. It is this flame that leads the steps of man to the Innermost Sanctuary—our "Home."

Chapter 11

LOVE AND JOY

HERE ARE THREE BASIC energies which, when used intelligently, make a man healthy, wealthy, and creative. These three energies are light, love, and will. Light and will combined produce joy. Every time your light and your willpower increase, you enter into a greater joy.

Enlightened people are always in continuous joy, because at the time of real enlightenment, the person comes in contact with the energy of willpower within his nature, and "the will aspect begins to control." Enlightenment expands the horizon of joy; willpower gives stability to joy. A joyful person radiates. All his actions on any level are creative, because the roots of his actions are extended into the realm of joy.

Joy combined with love produces the energy of healing, and the energy of attraction. In the presence of a loving and joyful person, creative possibilities bloom in your heart. You become magnetic

191

and attract all those who will work for you and for their own success. Your love and joy inspires them, charges them, and they give their utmost to increase the Source of their joy and love.

People search for joy and love, and when they find them, nothing can prevent sacrificing all that is necessary to support that Source of love and joy.

Love is our Essence. When we love, we release our Essence; and to live means to bring your Essence into expression, into release.

The only time that we really live is the time that we love, when our Inner Essence is in manifestation. The measure of our life is the measure of our love. You live as long as you love. If you "lived" ninety-five years, but loved only one year, you did not live for ninety-five years, but for only one year—not more. The rest was a waste of time. You can actually write on the tombstone of such a man:

"Here lies Mr. So and So. He was born in
1885
and passed away
in
1980
but he lived only one year.

People will be surprised. But never mind, for they will eventually realize that a life lived for one's own sake does not count. It is only the life lived for the service of others that counts. And such a life of service is a life of love and joy.

In loving, you release your Essential Self—the condensed and individualized life. Life is creative. It not only manifests through creative thoughts, feelings, and actions but also makes others creative and radioactive.

In every act of real love and real joy, you are manifesting your Inner Core. When your Essence is in operation, in expression, you are alive. You are alive when you express love.

Joy and love operate through our five senses on the physical, emotional, and mental planes. When the energy of joy and love operates through our five senses on the physical plane, it creates a happy man. Through all his senses, such a man enjoys the universe. His senses operate in their maximum capacity and transmit to him the thrill of the objective world.

It is your love and joy that transforms the world as you contact it with your five senses.

Nothing seems pleasant and delightful if the energy of love and joy does not flow through your senses and come in contact with the world of the five senses. Whatever you hear, touch, see, taste and smell, transmits your pleasure and happiness when you are full of love and joy.

The energy of love and joy on the emotional plane creates aspiration, ecstasy, fiery devotion, and one-pointedness in higher values.

In the mental plane, the energy of love and joy creates greater vision, creative striving, understanding, insight, foresight, synthetic perception, and creativity. Love and joy give power to your mind to penetrate into greater mysteries of higher contacts, and the ability to sustain your freedom in all your contacts.

The problems of the world can be solved by the energy of love and joy. Bring joy and love into the meetings at the United Nations, and the problems of the world will lose their control and gradually melt away.

Love and joy operate on higher planes too. For example, on the Intuitional Plane, love and joy create revelation. When you touch the network of Causes and blueprints, then all outer events are simplified in your loving and joy-radiating vision.

In the Atmic Plane, this energy of love and joy turns into power of will, enthusiasm, fearlessness, and command.

In the Monadic Plane, love unifies the man with the solar whole and joy pours down as a creative energy, purifying, energizing, enlightening, and impressing the Divine Beauty of higher realms.

On the Divine Plane, joy becomes a door through which flames of light, love, and power pass to cosmic dimensions.

Love and joy are the foundations of any creative and progressive work.

There is no real and true joy, if that joy is not imbued with love. Love cannot exist without joy.

The energy of love and joy:

1. Heals
2. Harmonizes
3. Expands
4. Creates magnetism

5. Reveals
6. Uplifts
7. Strengthens.

1. *Love and joy heal.* They heal physical, emotional, and mental wounds and sicknesses; align and integrate the physical and etheric centers; and purify the astral body building the way of sublimation for sacral and solar plexus centers.

Emotional attachment, low desires, glamor, and negative emotions are slowly washed away by the increasing energy of joy and love. If one exercises joy and love for half an hour daily, he will be a new man.

The energy of love and joy has a great effect on mental health. In a loving and joyful atmosphere, the mind gets sharper, clearer, with increasing power of insight and foresight. Love links a man with the realm of intuition. Joy builds the bridge toward Higher Will.

2. *Love and joy have a great harmonizing effect* on our physical, emotional, and mental nature; they create harmony in groups and raise their efficiency; they create harmony in nations and in humanity. Love and joy link humanity with greater centers of wisdom, light, and power.

Love and joy affect the animals and make them more protective and productive.

Love and joy affect the plant kingdom: trees, bushes, and vegetables. Give love and joy and your aura will nourish the vegetable kingdom, your trees will bear more fruit, and your flowers will be more fragrant.

3. *Love and joy are energies which cause expansion.* They expand your consciousness, your horizon, your inclusiveness. They expand the field of your spiritual influence.

Art uplifts and transforms people when they are charged with the energy of love and joy. A joyful expression of creative talent expands the understanding of people. An artwork full of love makes man touch higher dimensions.

4. *Love and joy charge our etheric, astral, and mental bodies with*

magnetism. Man's personality becomes a magnet, attracting higher ideas and visions as well as prana from the sun. The real assimilation of prana and food is at its highest when a person loves and is full of joy. Loving and joyful persons attract those who help them and support their service for humanity.

A joyful and loving person lives in abundance, enjoying the fruits of his labor. Many people make money but they do not enjoy it until love and joy fill their hearts.

5. *Love and joy slowly remove the veils, walls and hindrances between people, and establish contact and communion.* People reveal themselves when they feel that you love them, when they feel that you have joy in your heart. Love and joy create great trust and allow you to see things in people you have never seen. Through love and joy, the causes of problems are seen and handled in the right way. Love removes barriers existing between people. Joy removes barriers between the planes.

6. *Joy and love uplift people.* As we increase our love and joy, step by step, we raise the focus of our consciousness, we raise our social status, we raise our love, we uplift our hearts and our minds from the petty problems of life, and fill our hearts with the inspiration for our future achievements.

Extend your hand with joy and love, and people will grasp it and lift themselves from their common troubles and anxieties. Approach the sick with love and joy and their tonality will change and raise. Speak with joy and love and you will uplift masses.

7. *Joy is a tonic for nerves.* Love purifies the blood and strengthens the heart.

Joy and love are great shields against psychic attacks, against dark forces. Negative and dark forces hate joy, and cannot breathe in the fragrance of love.

Love and joy strengthen a group, a society, a nation, and make them invincible.

Before you eat or drink, charge your food or water with love and joy and you will notice a great difference in your health. Before you speak, before you try to serve, charge yourself with love and joy and you will see how people are elevated and strengthened.

The radiation of love reveals greater depths of your nature. With these greater depths, greater joy flows out. As you love, you reveal your Innermost Essence. Through your own Essence, the Essence of the Great Mystery dawns in your heart.

Love and joy are carriers of Divine Purpose. "God is Love." In loving you will meet God. Without love, one will never understand the Plan and Purpose of God.

To understand love and joy, we must try to experience them. Any time we think we love, we must try to know the level of our love ,and its motive. It may be physical love, emotional love, mental love, or higher love. It can be personal love, group love, national love, global love, or a love for Infinity.

As the level of love rises, and the motive behind it becomes more inclusive, your consciousness expands, and your understanding deepens in the same degree.

The same thing must be done with our joy. See where your joy lies, where it starts and where it ends. Find the causes of you joy and try to clearly see the level where it originated.

After seeing a few levels of your joy, try to raise the level of your joy and make it more inclusive, to the point where you feel joy for the whole existence. After such a stage of joy, you become a flow of love and joy.

The energy of love and joy can manifest on any level of human existence. As the level is raised, through which the energy of love and joy expresses itself, you receive a deeper and better response from the world. Your deeper joy evokes a deeper joy from others. Your deeper love evokes a deeper love from others. Eventually, one reaches a stage where love and joy fuse with the love and joy of millions. This fusion opens the gates of the future for humanity and protects humanity from wrong or self-destructive actions.

"The measure of understanding is the degree of love . . . love above all attracts the fire of space . . . As a lever sets the wheels in motion, so love sets up the strongest reaction. Compared with the radiance of love, the strongest hatred reflects only as a hideous mark. For love is the true reality and treasure."[1]

"*The measure of understanding is the degree of love . . . love above all attracts the fire of space . . .*" The fire of space is the love contained in the space in which we live and move and have our being. When you keep loving, your love increases, raising its level to such a degree that, eventually, you become a total sacrifice for humanity. The fire of space consumes you. The fire of love consumes you. Nothing remains in you, except love—a total love for Life and all its forms.

The fire of space consumes all that is attached to you, but you are not annihilated. You, as a drop, become the ocean. Just one second of realization of this blessed state, takes away all fears and you shine with the love of life.

"As a lever sets the wheels in motion, so love sets up the strongest reaction." Your love deepens and increases as the reaction to your love increases. Ingratitude, betrayals of various forms, hatred, action taken to destroy your reputation and labor, are reactions to

; open the way of your love's ray to pour out abundantly. Eventually, reaction turns into a response.

Love and joy work miracles in those conditions where there is a lack of love and joy. That is why the enemy must be respected, because he freely works for your improvement and perfection.

"Compared with the radiance of love, the strongest hatred reflects only as a hideous mark. For love is the true reality and treasure." The radiance of love increases as you love more. Love, if used continuously on one level, without trying to use it on higher levels, eventually becomes your enemy, and burns your mechanism. The safest way to use love energy is to continuously make efforts to use it on higher and higher levels and planes as the need arises.

If a person has one level of love and there is no striving to raise this level, you get tired of that person and look for one who can love with you on many levels and planes, or on all planes if necessary.

If love does not increase, it decreases and turns into a negative force. Love only exists in its process of expansion. Decreasing love turns into hatred, into self-interest, into "mine" and "yours," into anger, violence, jealousy, and eventually into apathy and inertia.

". . . Two thousand years ago it was pointed out that Fire would devour the Earth. Many thousands of years ago the Patriarchs warned humanity of the fiery peril. Science has failed to pay attention to many signs. No one is willing to think on a planetary scale. Thus We speak before the awesome time. One may still not escape the last hour. Help can be extended, but hatred will not be a healer.[2]

The "awesome time" is in front of us. It is the atomic war; it is natural cataclysm; it is depression; it is hatred; it is unemployment; it is the degeneration of morals; it is the increase of crime, drug abuse, pollution, etc. When the result of all these is combined you have the "awesome time"—the Armageddon of the seers.

Scientists have kept themselves busy flooding the market with their inventions, but they have given little attention to the increasing pollution belt around the planet. We are told that this five to ten mile accumulation of gases can one day ignite and catch on fire, and the planet with all its scientists, can burn to ashes. No one will be saved if this madness of playing with nature continues.

Before that awesome hour, it is possible to change the direction of life through love and joy which will lead the planet into sanity, health, purity, and beauty. To work for the welfare of one humanity, we must check our lives and see if there is an increasing joy and love behind all that we think, feel, and do.

One day a beloved lawyer friend told me, "I worked day and night and became a money machine. There is no love and joy in such a mechanical life."

I told him that there are millions of people like him, and the only way to escape such a mechanical life is to introduce joy into all his thoughts, feelings and actions, and start doing things as a loving service for others.

We know that the planet and humanity can be saved with the heroic efforts of those who love this planet and who love humanity. ". . . No creative attainment, no cooperation, in fact no community is possible without magnanimity. One can observe how through magnanimity labor is made tenfold easier and, it would seem, nothing could be simpler during an inspired work than to wish only for the good and for success of one's neighbor! Joy is the result of manifested labor. Joy is a great helper."[3]

Labor is striving to change the life, and make the planet a better place to live.

Labor is striving to make people love more, to make their love inclusive. Through such a labor, joy is released and manifested. Joy inspires you to carry on your labor in spite of all adverse conditions. Each true labor increases your joy, and joy increases your enthusiasm to labor more.

Magnanimity is the ability to stand above all adverse conditions in great love and joy. It is the ability to carry your labor with vision and with the inspiration of the Future.

Magnanimity is great spiritual solemnity and dignity of the spirit. It is the royal grandeur of the Inner Divine Self.

It is magnanimity that radiates the solemn joy, the profound love that persists in all adverse conditions.

"Joy lies within itself and has first of all, the quality of directness, straight-forwardness and a smile for everything. Precisely joy helps to bridge over all hostile obstacles. Joy is one of the best means for the overcoming of hostile attacks. . . . Joy is always the shortest path to exaltation . . ."[4]

This is so beautiful. One can use the above quotation for a year as a seed thought for meditation. Great Sages advised their students to meditate on joy, and measure their daily life by the standards of joy. Exaltation of the human spirit can be seen only in a joy flaming with love. Joy transforms our being and lifts us closer to our essence.

"Speaking of the kinds of love, let us note the love that holds back and the love that inspires. In essence the first love is earthly, and the second heavenly. But what a multitude of constructive efforts were destroyed by the first! And a similar multitude winged by the second! The first is aware of all the limitations of space and consciousness; but the second has no need of earthly measurements. . . . The second love embraces the physical world and the Subtle and Fiery Worlds as well. It kindles hearts for the highest joy and is thus indestructible. Thus, let us expand the heart—not for Earth but for Infinity."[5]

People "expand their heart for the Earth," to possess the Earth, and eventually find out that they are possessed by the Earth. Thus, joy disappears. Thus, love disappears. The Earth absorbs them.

When people expand their hearts toward Infinity or spiritual values, the Earth itself offers its beauty and love, and helps men to climb toward their true destination. We are told that owning the Earth is not our destination. Earth is a station along the path toward Infinity. Those who are possessed by the Earth will remain with it, as a passenger dropped out of the train.

". . . It is useful to impregnate space with joy, and very dangerous to strew the heavens with sorrow. . . . Joy is the health of the spirit."[6]

"*It is useful to impregnate space with joy.*" We seldom realize that as we think, feel and act, we inject various kinds of substance into space. Joy is a substance, fear is another substance. Love, hate and gratitude are different kinds of substances. It is necessary to ask ourselves what kind of substance are we dumping into the space?

Space can be polluted with the substance of illusions, glamors, and wrong motives. Such substances contaminate people, who because of their various weaknesses, draw these substances into their mechanism.

It is also important to know that each human being has a space— a sphere around his body. This sphere can expand or contract. It expands if the substance you are injecting into the greater space is in the nature of love, joy, and beauty. But, if the substance you are injecting is in the nature of hatred, base thoughts, crimes, then you gradually narrow your space and bury yourself in your own negative and deadly substance. Many sicknesses of the mind, heart and body are the result of a narrowing sphere around you.

As your sphere expands through right thoughts, right action and loving conditions, through joy and love, you penetrate into greater space and draw much finer living energy, light, love and power into your system.

The substance of joy is a great nourishment, a great tonic and inspiration for those who are striving on the path of service, on the path of enlightenment, and on the path of conscious evolution.

Our aura, impregnated with joy, is a colorful symphony with great magnetism.

We often impregnate our rooms, our gardens, our offices with worries, with negative feelings, with destructive thoughtforms of various kinds. The sphere around our dwelling and working places gets so contaminated with such pollution that our sul has a hard time to breathe and to be creative.

Instead of such negative substances, we can fill our homes and offices with the substance of joy and love, and thus increase our vitality, creativity and service for the world.

There was a depressed girl who worked in one of the post offices near my home. She looked very sad. One day, instead of talking to her, I looked at her and smiled.

"What do you want?" she asked.

"A stamp."

"How many and what kind?"

"Three ten cent stamps." I paid for the stamps and said to her, "You know, your eyes . . . oh, never mind."

"What about my eyes?"

"Your eyes . . ."

"Come on, what is it?"

"I can't tell you now . . . ," and I left.

Next week, I waited until my turn came. She was looking and waiting for me.

"Two ten cent stamps, please."

"What about my eyes?"

"You know, I want to tell you a secret."

"Oh, come on."

"When you smile, your eyes are so beautiful, but if you keep looking sad, your eyes look like the eyes of a witch."

"Is it really so?"

"Yes, try always to smile and you will be so beautiful." She gave me a big smile and I departed.

Every time after that she gave me a bigger smile. Five months later, she disappeared. I asked another clerk,

"Where is she?"

"Your smiling girl?"

"Yes."

"She was promoted. She is working in the office. You changed her life."

"May I see her?"

"Yes."

He went to inform her. She came out and hugged me and with a most beautiful smile said,

"The day you taught me to smile, a joy sprang out of my heart. I am happy now. Thank you for what you did for me."

Let us impregnate space with joy. Start with a smile and the rest will slowly follow.

". . . (it is) *very dangerous to strew the heavens with sorrow. Joy is the health of the spirit.*" A space stratified with sorrow is a space through which destructive and negative forces operate. Even germs like a space full of sorrow; they grow there more abundantly. Dark forces like depression and sorrow because they can easily control a person caught by sorrow and depression. Sorrow blocks the vision of the future, devitalizes your body and paralyzes your intellect.

". . . The successful mastery of all trials lies within our hearts and consists in our love for the Lord. If we are filled with love, can obstacles exist? Earthly love itself creates miracles. Does not the fiery love for Hierarchy multiply our forces? . . ."[7]

We are told that the disciples came to Christ and said, "How will they know that we are your disciples?" They were waiting for Him to say, "You will be a colonel. You will be a king. You will be a queen, and people will know that you are . . ."

He answered, "The world will know that you are my disciples when you love each other." I believe He meant to say that if you really love each other and do not let that love go, making that love deeper and deeper, they will know that you are my disciples, because I am manifested Love. You can witness love only by being love. People will know if you are expressing, living or manifesting the substance—the love that I brought you. But if you hate each other, if you create separativeness, you are not my disciples!

The greatest love and joy exist among those people who really serve the Lord and the Hierarchy. Their love is permanent, and their joy ever increases.

Striving toward the Lord pulls the human soul out of personality problems and relationships, and raises it closer to the core of the spirit. The closer one goes to his true Self, the greater are the radiations of joy and love.

Man charges himself with energy when he dedicates his life to an ideal.

"It is said, 'Do not enter Fire in inflammable garments, but bring a fiery joy.' In this indication lies the entire prerequisite for communion with the Fiery World. Verily, even the garments of the Subtle World are not always suitable for the Fiery World. So, too, the joy of ascent must transcend any earthly joy. . . . Even in the flowers of Earth, in the plumage of birds, and in the wonders of the heavens, one can find that very joy which prepares one for the gates of the Fiery World."[8]

"Inflammable garments" are those vehicles, namely: physical, emotional, and mental which are full of pollution of various kinds. Increasing energy from higher spheres burns your vehicles if they are not pure. Only a purified vehicle can stand the pressure and the fire of the higher planes.

Fiery joy purifies the vehicles, makes them "fire-proof." Fiery joy eliminates the vices of your bodies. Once they are purified from earthbound tendencies, they turn into channels of pure love, beauty, goodness, and truth. It is only by purified garments that one can stand in the presence of a Great One, or enter His Ashram.

Love and joy increase on each step of our ascent toward the Lord, toward the vision. Only a life dedicated to human welfare witnesses the joy of ascent. Joy and love increase in our heart to such a degree that we eventually get ready to sacrifice all that we are, all that we have for the service of the one Life.

There are twelve main obstacles of love and joy. If you conquer or avoid these obstacles, your love and joy will increase.

The first obstacle is *pressure*. Any time you exercise pressure on others, or try to force your will upon the will of others, love and joy weaken and eventually disappear. Love and joy increase only in a state of freedom.

People even try to use pressure with their thoughts, ideas, visions, dreams and art, but eventually they realize that a growing rejection is accumulating against them. True joy and love do not need pressure. Radiate your love. Radiate your joy. Radiate your beauty. Let us not use any form of pressure. True friends and co-workers are those who come to you because of their free choice. Forced friendship eventually becomes a source of sorrow.

The second obstacle is *jealousy*. Jealousy saps the energy of love and joy. It burns the tissues of etheric, astral and mental vehicles and dissipates love and joy. Jealousy wants to possess and whoever possesses anything eventually loses his love and his joy. He loses his life.

A jealous person acts as an unconscious agent for dark forces. Jealousy prevents growth of joy and love between people. It destroys the seeds of future accomplishments.

The third obstacle is the *denial of freedom* of other persons. Such a violation literally extinguishes the flame of your love and joy. Only in freedom does joy increase and love bloom. Let the one you love be free. In his or her freedom find your joy. Let that person decide or plan and follow his own conscience, use his own free will. If you keep such an attitude, not only to your closest ones, but to all people, you will see the increase of love and joy in your heart.

Respect the ideas, the visions of others; be tolerant and make them respect your ideas and visions. If your ideas and visions are more inclusive, you will increase your love and joy.

The fourth obstacle of joy and love is the tendency to *misuse people and their belongings*. With such a tendency, love and joy eventually evaporate, because the spirit of exploitation rests in your heart.

There were two friends, a boy and girl. They were in love and joyful. One day, the boy asked the girl,

"How much do you make monthly?"

"Nine hundred dollars."

"You are really a darling. I love you so much. You know how much I love you, don't you?"

"Yes, I do."

"I want to go to school, and if you support me for five years, I will become a lawyer and then take care of you."

The girl hesitated, but because of her emotions she agreed, and they married. They had two children before the boy graduated from law school. The girl did her best to support her husband. After he graduated he came to me to speak about his graduation.

"How beautiful. You did it! And your wife was a heroine. For five years she supported you . . ."

"But," he said, "I would like to leave her."

"Leave her, for whom?"

"Just a divorce."

"But . . ."

"I am falling in love with someone else."

"Really?"

"Yes."

"What does your wife think?"

"I don't know. She is a little concerned."

"But for five years she supported you."

"Yes . . . but . . ."

They were divorced and he found the ways and means to pay

minimum support for the children. Often he would come to my office and I would ask him,

"Are you happy?"

"Sort of. I like this girl. We have great fun, but there is something in me that is closed. I can't love. I am not joyful and she senses it . . ."

"You cannot manipulate or use people with love," I said, "because the fountain of love goes dry without sacrifice, sincerity, and loyalty." I never saw him again.

The fifth obstacle is *non-inclusiveness*. Non-inclusiveness is a great enemy of love and joy. Love and joy are like fragrances. They expand and spread. Non-inclusiveness creates barriers and walls in your inner world.

Inclusiveness opens the path of expansion. Joy and love cannot be caged. They must flow and expand. Inclusiveness leads to right human relations, to international understanding, to respect, and appreciation.

Non-inclusiveness is self-worship, separation, which eventually breeds aggressiveness, hate, and conflict. Joy and love disappear in an atmosphere of separation. Once they disappear, hate and depression take their place.

The sixth obstacle is *unrighteousness*. If you are unrighteous in your thoughts, emotional responses, and actions you will not have real joy in your heart, and love will never bloom in you.

Joy and love increase when you respect the rights of other people. Those people who were not righteous to others carry a heavy burden in their conscience, and eventually that burden turns into a pressure and expresses itself through various sicknesses and complications in their lives.

A righteous man has joy and love even if people do not understand him.

The seventh obstacle for joy and love is *ugliness*. Beauty increases joy and love. Ugliness makes them disappear. Your love and joy fade away when you experience an ugly thought, emotion, action, or any ugly expression. Your thoughts are ugly when they are selfish, harmful, criminal, separative, false, etc. Your emotions are ugly when they are negative, when they lack solemnity. Your actions and expressions are ugly when they are destructive, insulting, belittling, and motivated by self-interest.

As one removes ugliness from his surroundings, from his thoughts, emotional reactions and actions, joy fills his heart and love increases in him. Beauty always shines in joy and love.

The eighth obstacle is *insincerity*. No love or joy exists in a heart which has an insincere attitude toward other human beings. Love and joy cannot exist where sincerity is absent. An insincere man eventually finds his love and joy fading away. Insincerity causes disintegration in mental substance, and severs the thread between the Inner Guide and man. To have joy and love one must strive with all his heart to be sincere and honest with the world.

The ninth obstacle of joy and love is *nosiness*. A nosy person cannot increase his love and joy. He is always occupied with personality affairs. He criticizes and judges. He interferes with the decisions of others, mentally or verbally. He evokes reactions and involvement with the personal lives of others.

Love does not like nosiness. Joy does not live where there is imposition of thoughts and manners.

Nosiness increases your worries and hurts other people. A nosy person cannot gain his freedom. Often he is caught in the net of gossip.

The tenth obstacle is *criticism*. Criticism creates rejection. Your aura hardens in its periphery. Every time you criticize you impose yourself on others. You impose your personality on others. Your personality grows thick in such a way that your Soul hardly finds a chance to shine out.

Criticism does not let other people experience and experiment. It does not let them grow and be themselves. Criticism presents and imposes its own molds and wants everyone to be molded by its standards. Thus, it limits the horizons and striving of others.

Love and joy cannot grow and expand in an atmosphere of criticism. Love and joy exist for all. When you hurt someone, you hurt your love and your joy.

The eleventh obstacle of joy and love is *carelessness* and *pride*. The two go together. Love cares. Joy communicates and identifies with the soul of others, with the success and achievements of others.

Carelessness leads one to irresponsibility. Where the sense of responsibility does not exist, there is no conscious love and real joy. Love and joy are two great pillars of light which lead people toward spirituality, toward universality, toward the highest values of life.

They cannot exist in a polluted atmosphere of human weaknesses and vices.

Pride is separative. Love is wholeness. Pride belittles others. Love and joy stand for the beauty and the interest of others.

People think that love and joy are personal properties. They are not personal properties. They are like sunshine, like air, like the fragrance of the hills. They belong to all or they do not exist. Pride repels all joy and love.

The twelfth obstacle of love and joy is *attachment*. You attach to something or somebody and say, "I love her, him, or it." But eventually you will be surprised when you try to make it your property and own it for your own enjoyment, for you will slowly lose your love and joy.

Attachment to any love-object makes you lose your joy, and your love for that object will bring great disappointment. One cannot hold the object of his love and joy. Only through non-attachment to your love-object, can you perpetuate your love and joy.

Love increases when you give love and let people love the way they want. You increase your joy by increasing the pure joy of others. You cannot run after love and joy. They are within you, and everywhere. In searching for love and joy you lose yourself. In being love and joy, you find your true Self.

Joy and love create an element in our etheric body and precipitate a kind of substance in our nerve channels which melts the poisons accumulated in our system through irritation, sorrow, depression and other negative emotions, thoughts or actions.

Lastly, joy and love expand the field of our magnetism within our aura, and we receive inspiration and impressions from Higher Realms, Galaxies and Great Existences.

Such a contact extremely enriches your creative abilities.

Those who live in the light of beauty, joy, love, freedom, live in the future, and create a culture which will evoke the best creative powers from coming generations. That is how the path of perfection for humanity is paved toward greater achievement, and toward greater health and bliss.

"Indeed, in every striving to the summits, in every ascent, is contained an untold joy. An inner impulse irresistibly calls people towards the heights."⁹

NOTES

Notes to Chapter 1

1. Roerich, Nicholas K., *Roerich Adamant*, p. 83.
2. Agni Yoga Society, *Leaves of Morya's Garden I*, para. 252.
3. *Ibid.*, para. 45.
4. *Ibid.*, para. 45.
5. *Ibid.*, para. 51.
6. *Ibid.*, para. 145.
7. *Ibid.*, para. 181.
8. *Ibid.*, para. 193.
9. *Ibid.*, para. 202.
10. *Ibid.*, para. 202.
11. *Ibid.*, para. 229.
12. *Ibid.*, para. 252.
13. *Ibid.*, para. 229.
14. *Ibid.*, para. 271.
15. St. Luke 23:24

Notes to Chapter 2

1. Agni Yoga Society, *New Era Community*, para. 1.
2. Agni Yoga Society, *Heart*, para. 1.

Notes to Chapter 3

1. Agni Yoga Society, *Fiery World I*, para. 190.
2. Saraydarian, Torkom, *The Legend of Shamballa*, p. 52.
3. Roerich, Nicholas K., *Roerich Adamant*, p. 16.
4. Agni Yoga Society, *Leaves of Morya's Garden I*, para. 333.
5. *Ibid.*, para. 271.
6. Agni Yoga Society, *Leaves of Morya's Garden II*, p. 199.
7. Agni Yoga Society, *Agni Yoga*, para. 15.
8. Roerich, Nicholas K., *Abode of Light*, p. 35.
9. Agni Yoga Society, *Fiery World I*, para. 177.
10. Agni Yoga Society, *Hierarchy*, para. 72.
11. Roerich, Nicholas K., *Roerich Adamant*, p. 95.
12. Agni Yoga Society, *Leaves of Morya's Garden I*, para. 252.
13. Agni Yoga Society, *Fiery World I*, para. 190.
14. *Ibid.*, para. 190.
15. Roerich, Nicholas K., *Himavat*, p. 233.
16. Agni Yoga Society, *Hierarchy*, para. 249.
17. *Ibid.*, para. 146.

Notes to Chapter 4

1. Agni Yoga Society, *Agni Yoga*, para. 51.
2. *Ibid.*, para. 336.
3. Agni Yoga Society, *Aum*, para. 150.

Notes to Chapter 5

1. Bailey, Alice A., *A Treatise on White Magic*, p. 117.
2. Bailey, Alice A., *A Treatise on Cosmic Fire*, p. 755.
3. Agni Yoga Society, *Leaves of Morya's Garden I*, para. 27.
4. Gen. 25:29-34

Notes to Chapter 6

1. Agni Yoga Society, *Agni Yoga*, para. 424.
2. *Ibid.*, para. 424.
3. Agni Yoga Society, *Hierarchy*, para. 105.

Notes to Chapter 7

1. Agni Yoga Society, *Hierarchy*, para. 280.
2. I Corinthians 13:1-13

Notes to Chapter 9

1. See Bailey, Alice A., *Glamour: A World Problem*, pp. 121-123.

Notes to Chapter 10

1. Agni Yoga Society, *Fiery World II*, para. 258.
2. Bhagavad Gita, *translated by H. Saraydarian*, Ch. II, Verse 23-24.
3. Agni Yoga Society, *Fiery World I*, para. 298.
4. Agni Yoga Society, *Fiery World II*, para. 110.
5. Agni Yoga Society, *Agni Yoga*, para. 459.

Notes to Chapter 11

1. Agni Yoga Society, *Agni Yoga*, para. 424.
2. Agni Yoga Society, *Fiery World II*, para. 9.
3. Agni Yoga Society, *Fiery World III*, para. 424.
4. Roerich, Nicholas K., *Abode of Light*, p. 41.
5. Agni Yoga Society, *Heart*, para. 242.
6. Agni Yoga Society, *Fiery World I*, para. 298.
7. *Ibid.*, para. 637.
8. *Ibid.*, para. 638.
9. Roerich, Nicholas K., *Himavat*, p. 12.